CRAFTING WOODEN LAMPS

KEN BURTON

POPULAR WOODWORKING BOOKS
CINCINNATI, OHIO
www.popularwoodworking.com

READ THIS IMPORTANT SAFETY NOTICE

To prevent accidents, keep safety in mind while you work. Use the safety guards installed on power equipment; they are for your protection.

When working on power equipment, keep fingers away from saw blades, wear safety goggles to prevent injuries from flying wood chips and sawdust, wear hearing protection and consider installing a dust vacuum to reduce the amount of airborne sawdust in your woodshop.

Don't wear loose clothing, such as neckties or shirts with loose sleeves, or jewelry, such as rings, necklaces or bracelets, when working on power equipment. Tie back long hair to prevent it from getting caught in your equipment.

People who are sensitive to certain chemicals should check the chemical content of any product before using it.

Due to the variability of local conditions, construction materials, skill levels, etc., neither the author nor Popular Woodworking Books assumes any responsibility for any accidents, injuries, damages or other losses incurred resulting from the material presented in this book.

The authors and editors who compiled this book have tried to make the contents as accurate and correct as possible. Plans, illustrations, photographs and text have been carefully checked. All instructions, plans and projects should be carefully read, studied and understood before beginning construction.

Prices listed for supplies and equipment were current at the time of publication and are subject to change.

METRIC CONVERSION CHART

to convert	to	multiply by
Inches	Centimeters	2.54
Centimeters	Inches	0.4
Feet	Centimeters	30.5
Centimeters	Feet	0.03
Yards	Meters	0.9
Meters	Yards	1.1

Distributed in Canada by Fraser Direct
100 Armstrong Avenue
Georgetown, Ontario L7G 5S4
Canada

Distributed in the U.K. and Europe by F&W Media International LTD
Brunel House, Ford Close
Newton Abbot
TQ12 4PU, UK
Tel: (+44) 1626 323200
Fax: (+44) 1626 323319
E-mail: enquiries@fwmedia.com

Distributed in Australia by Capricorn Link
P.O. Box 704
Windsor, NSW 2756
Australia

Visit our Web site at www.popularwoodworking.com.

Other fine Popular Woodworking Books are available from your local bookstore or direct from the publisher.

15   14   13   12   11   5   4   3   2   1

ACQUISITIONS EDITOR: David Thiel
DESIGNER: Brian Roeth
PRODUCTION COORDINATOR: Mark Griffin
PHOTOGRAPHER: Ken Burton
ILLUSTRATOR: Jim Stack

ABOUT THE AUTHOR

Ken Burton has been working with wood professionally for the past thirty or so years. After more than a decade of playing in his father's basement shop, he got his formal start through the Fine Woodworking program at Bucks County Community College. From there he collected a Bachelor's degree in Industrial Arts Education at Millersville University of Pennsylvania and a Master of Fine Arts in Woodworking and Furniture Design from the School for American Crafts at the Rochester Institute of Technology. At this point, he is pretty seriously over-educated for a woodworker.

Currently, Ken operates Windy Ridge Woodworks in New Tripoli, PA where he designs and builds studio furniture, custom cabinetry and accessories.

In the summer months you can often find him teaching woodworking workshops at the Yestermorrow Design/Build School in Warren, Vermont or at Peters Valley Craft Center in Layton, NJ.

Ken is father to two girls: Sarah, and Emma and is enjoying sharing his love of making things with them. One of Emma's latest projects is a balloon popper which she designed after seeing one in a picture in one of her books.

Despite a huge backlog of projects, Ken generally answers his e-mail in a timely manner. You can contact him through his website: www.wrwoodworks.com.

ACKNOWLEDGEMENTS

The roots of this book run deep, so allow me to say thank you to those people who have encouraged me along the way. I have been quite fortunate to have been taught by some of the finest craftsmen in the country: Jon Alley and Mark Sfirri of BCCC; George Hauber of Millersville University, Bill Keyser, Doug Sigler, and John Dodd of RIT among others.

Thanks too, to the women in my life who have put up with me while I was pulling this whole project together: daughters Sarah and Emma and my partner Janet who has come to mean so much.

And a special shout-out to the crew at F+W Media including David Thiel who managed to put together a great looking publication despite my efforts to miss every deadline.

And finally thanks to Susie Thibodeau and the Asheville-Schoonmaker Mica Co. for being kind enough to supply me with Mica and walk me through the process of how to use it.

DEDICATION

For Emma Janelle Burton who has brightened my life more than any lamp ever could.

TABLE OF CONTENTS

INTRODUCTION

MAKING LAMPS IS A GREAT MIX of fine woodworking and mechanical construction, of art and engineering, of aesthetics and practicality. Whether you're building your first lamp, or your hundred-and-first, there are design challenges to overcome and electrical problems to solve: How will you fasten a socket to that lovely piece of burl, Where will the wires run through that graceful bend? How will the thing be turned on and off? Coming up with creative and effective answers to these questions is part of the fun of designing and building wooden lamps.

One of the first things you come up against with lamp design is that there is not a lot of historic precedent. The incandescent light bulb (which made electric lamps possible) wasn't really "perfected" until the latter part of the 19th century. By this time, quite a few furniture styles had come and gone from fashion. So if you're looking to devise an electric lamp to fit in with your Chippendale-inspired living room suite, you're not going to find a lot of antique examples to copy. Candle holders, maybe, but no electric lamps. So, you'll need to improvise, picking up on some of the design motifs from the period you're trying to emulate.

As I was growing up, I watched my father do just this as he made lamps for a furniture shop that specialized in colonial pine furniture. By picking up on some of the detailing and proportions of the other furniture in the genre, my father was able to make a number of different designs that looked quite in keeping with the other period pieces despite their incorporation of relatively new technology.

Speaking of technology, one of the next things you run into as you design a lamp is how to deal with imperfect technology. You may have noticed I put the word "perfected" in quotation marks earlier when I mentioned incandescent lights. This is because despite better than 100 years of development, the incandescent light bulb is far from perfect. Sure, it has its pluses: it is cheap and gives off a lot of light. But it also has some rather significant negatives: it isn't very efficient in its use of energy — it gives off plenty of heat

along with the light it produces, and the light it produces is rather harsh. So lamp designs have evolved over the years to deal with these shortcomings. They use shades to temper and diffuse the light and these shades are often designed to dissipate or at least to not trap heat. Unfortunately, there is not a lot that a lamp designer can do to help out with the energy efficiency of a bulb other than to specify the use of a more efficient one. Fortunately, we have some good options to this end. Compact florescent bulbs are much more efficient than incandescents in many applications. Part of this efficiency can be seen (felt?) in how cool they remain when lit. There are also significant advances being made in LED technology to the point where some LED bulbs are now available for general, ambient lighting purposes.

As for the lamps in this book, their designs are pretty eclectic. In general, wooden lamps tend to be somewhat less formal than their polished metal counterparts. But there are degrees of informality. Some of my lamps, such as Victor, make use of some very traditional furniture elements and will blend right into a more formally furnished room. Others are a bit more whimsical. David's lamp, for example, picks up on the idea that a floor lamp can have an almost human appearance.

As you contemplate which of the designs to tackle, I encourage you to step out of your comfort zone both aesthetically and technically and to try something new. Wander the aisles of your local hardware store or home center. As I was putting this book together, that is what I did and I found some great new materials with which to work. In particular, I came across a selection of glass blocks which formed the inspiration for three of the lamps herein (Lighthouse, Harlequin, and Deco). Build any of my lamps as presented, or modify them to suit your purposes. When you get finished shoot a few pictures and e-mail them to me. I'd love to see what you are up to. Good luck and enjoy building some lamps.

KEN BURTON | WINDY RIDGE WOODWORKS | NEW TRIPOLI, PA

THE DREADED
ELECTRICAL CHAPTER

THE NAME OF THIS CHAPTER is a little tongue in cheek, but it has a certain amount of truth in it. Many of the woodworkers I've talked to are a little reluctant to make lamps simply because they perceive the wiring to be a problem. This is a reasonable concern, especially if you haven't done any wiring before. The purpose of this chapter is to allay those fears and to show you that lamp wiring is actually pretty simple.

This is not to say that the wiring part should be taken lightly. You don't have to read too many news stories about house fires to find out that faulty wiring is often to blame. However, when done correctly, a lamp you make and wire yourself is just as safe as one that comes from a manufacturer. The key is to take your time and make sure all the connections are done properly. If you are ever in doubt about what you are doing, consult with a licensed electrician.

Lamp Parts

Most well-stocked hardware stores and home centers will have the parts needed to make the lamps in this book. If you make more than one or two lamps, you may find it more economical to seek out an electrical supplier, or to go online to a specialty website such as www.mylampparts.com.

As you start putting your lamps together, you may notice that these parts are a little different than the kind of hardware typical of furniture-making. There are some funny names involved, and the way the pieces are threaded is pretty much only compatible with other lamp parts. A lot of this goes back to the early days of electricity when gas lamps were being replaced with incandescent bulbs. In many cases the light fixtures weren't replaced, but were reworked to adapt to

In a typical lamp, you'll be using these parts (from top to bottom) Finial, Harp, Socket, Hex Nut, Bottom Clamp, Nipple, Hex Nut, Lamp Cord. A few lamps also make use of a Line Switch.

Lamp sockets consist of four parts (from top to bottom): Shell, Insulator, Socket Interior, and Base.

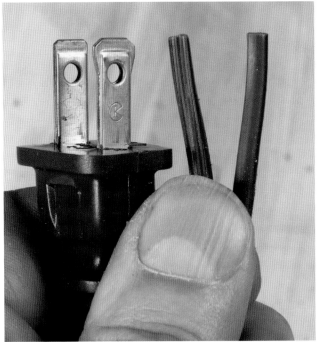

Lamp cord has a polarized plug at one end and two conductors to connect to the lamp socket. Note that the insulation on one of the conductors is ribbed. This is the wire that connects to the neutral side of the circuit.

the new technology. Thus the threads of the new sockets and whatnot had to match that of the old gas lines. These days it is pretty rare to find gas light fixtures in a house, but the threading of the various bits and pieces carries on as a legacy of the nineteenth century.

The photo on the opposite page shows the parts typical of the lamps in this book. Central to most of the lamps is a threaded steel tube, which is often plated with brass. This is called lamp tube. A short length of lamp tube is usually referred to as a nipple. Lamp tube comes in four diameters: ⅛ IP, ¼ IP, ⅜ IP, and ¼-27. Of the four, ⅛ IP is the most common. The IP stands for "iron pipe" The sizes refer to the Briggs Standard of Wrought-Iron Pipe Dimensions, which came about in the 19th century. ⅛ IP nipples have 27 threads per inch and so require special nuts and other adapters to fit. Their outside diameter is 0.405" which is an easy fit in a ⁷⁄₁₆" hole, and a snug fit in a ¹³⁄₃₂" hole. (Most of the plans in this book specify ¹³⁄₃₂".) ¼ IP and ⅜ IP lamp tube are larger in diameter than ⅛ IP, while ¼-27 is smaller. Lamp tube provides a passage way for the lamp's wiring, as well as a means of fastening the electrical components to the lamp's structure.

The lamp socket is the part that holds the light bulb. Sockets usually consist of four parts as shown above left. The base (or shell base) has a threaded hole in the bottom that twists onto one end of a nipple. The upper rim of the base is crimped much like a pie

shell. This crimping engages with mating crimps in the shell — the socket's outer metal sleeve. Contained between the two pieces are a cardboard insulator which isolates the electrical connections from the shell and the socket interior — the part that actually holds the bulb and is where the wiring attaches. Most sockets include an on/off switch of some kind (push button, twist, pull chain) although you can get them without such.

The wire that delivers electricity from the wall to the socket is called a lamp cord. This kind of cord has a plug on one end that fits into the wall and two conductors that carry the current. These days most of the cords sold are polarized — which means they only fit into a wall socket one way. If you look closely at the plug shown above right, you'll see that one of the blades is wider than the other, This wide blade fits into the wider of the two slots in the wall receptacle.

To understand why this is important, you need to know a little about the wiring inside the walls of your house. Every wall receptacle is connected to the main electrical panel by a wire that contains three conductors: one with black insulation, one with white insulation, and one that is bare. The bare wire is the ground. It provides an alternative path for the electricity in case something malfunctions. As lamps usually aren't grounded, you don't really have to worry about the ground wire other than to know that it exists. Of the other two conductors, the black one is called the hot and the white one is the neutral. The wide blade on a lamp cord connects to the neutral side of the house's wiring.

If you look at two conductors that make up a lamp cord, you'll see the insulation on one side is ribbed. This is the neutral conductor that connects to the wider plug. (Some manufacturers put lettering or other markings on the neutral conductor rather than ribbing.) The other side is the hot conductor. It is important not to get these conductors mixed up. When you attach the wires to the socket, the neutral (ribbed) wire attaches to the silver screw and the hot (plain) wire gets connected to the brass screw. While the lamp will probably work if you switch the wires, the socket could potentially become a serious shock hazard. More on how to make the actual connections later.

The harp is a metal loop that holds the lamp shade in place. Harps range in size from 4" on up to 16" or more in ½" increments. When you go to purchase a shade for your lamp, take the lamp with you. This way you can match the size of the harp to the shade/base combination. The harp is held in place with a bottom clamp, a metal clip that looks a little like a large wing nut. At the top of the harp is a metal stud for the shade. These studs are typically threaded ¼-27. A finial screws to the stud to lock the shade in place. Note: not all shades require a harp, but I usually install a bottom clamp anyway, so the harp option is open should I want to use a different shade at a later time.

On a few of the lamps, the design doesn't allow for a socket that has a integral switch. For these, you'll need to get a line switch — a switch that can be wired directly on the lamp cord itself.

Low Voltage Lamps

A few of the lamps in the book make use of modular LED lights. These are low-voltage units that consist of a transformer that plugs into the wall, and one or more pucks that contain the LEDs as shown in the photos. The transformer converts the high voltage AC current that comes from the power company into the 12 volts DC that the LEDs need. LEDs are Light Emitting Diodes — semiconductors that produce light quite efficiently. While these kits often come with various connectors and switches, most of the time you'll be clipping these things off and using switches from Radio Shack that integrate better with the lamps' designs.

WARNING! In addition to LED puck lighting systems, there are also pucks that use halogen bulbs. These bulbs burn much hotter than LEDs. The lamps in this book are not designed to dissipate that kind of heat. Use only LED pucks. Do not use those with halogen bulbs.

Some of the lamp designs call for low voltage LED lights. These are sold in kits containing the necessary transformer along with one or more cylindrical lighting "pucks". These lights are turned on and off through rocker switches purchased at Radio Shack.

Tools

Wiring a lamp requires only a handful of tools, many of which you probably already have. As shown in the photo, these include screwdrivers (both straight and Phillips), needle nose pliers, wire strippers (which often include a wire cutter), a utility knife and a small crescent wrench. For wiring LED puck lights you'll also need to include a soldering iron.

Your electrical tool kit need not be very extensive. The only tools that are specific to electrical work are the wire strippers and the soldering iron.

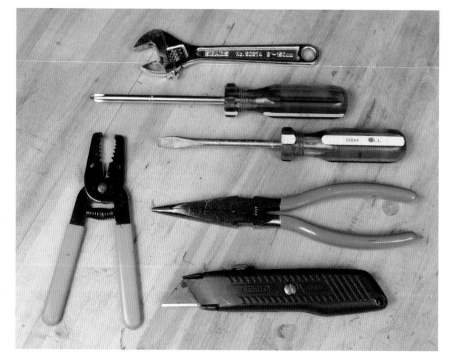

Wiring a Standard Lamp

Wiring a regular socket to the top of a lamp is partially a mechanical process and partly an electrical one. The mechanical process involves installing the nipple, socket, bottom clamp etc. while the electrical part consists of attaching the wires to the right places. Mostly it is a matter of doing things in the right order so you aren't stuck with something that should go through something else but can't because another piece is in the way.

Start by installing the nipple (and bottom clamp). These are held in place with two hex nuts. Leave about ½" of nipple extending beyond the clamp for the socket base to thread onto. Thread the base onto the nipple and lock it in place with its integral set screw as shown in the photo, below left.

Feed a length of lamp cord up through the nipple and out through the base. Split the cord into its two separate leads and tie the two together in what is called an underwriter's knot as shown in the photo at bottom right. This knot prevents the cord from pulling back out of the lamp. It also keeps tension off of the electrical connections.

Cut the leads if necessary, leaving yourself ends about 1½" long to work with. Strip about ½" of the insulation off each lead and roll the bare conductor between your thumb and forefinger to twist the individual strands together. Bend the end into a "U" shape so it can wrap around the terminal on the socket. Loosen the screw on the socket and wrap the hooked end of the wire around it in a clockwise manner as shown in the photo at bottom. Tighten the screw to lock the wire in place. Repeat with the other lead, fastening it to the socket's second screw. Note, to maintain proper polarity, the wire with the ribbed insulation should connect to the silver screw and the wire with the plain insulation should connect to the brass screw.

Slide the cardboard insulator and socket shell over the socket interior and press down until the crimps overlap and lock. Plug the lamp in and test the socket with a bulb.

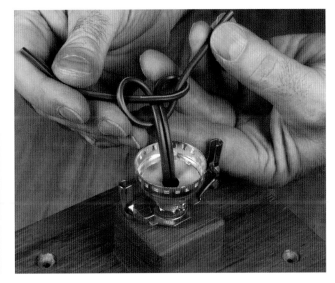

Most lamp sockets include a set screw that allows you to lock the unit in place after you have threaded it onto a piece of lamp pipe.

To keep the cord from pulling out of the socket, split the two leads and tie them together in an underwriter's knot.

When making wire connections, be sure there is no bare wire exposed below the screw. Also, be sure the wire wraps around the screw in a clockwise manner so the action of tightening the screw doesn't loosen the connection.

IT'S NOT THE HUMIDITY, IT'S THE HEAT.

Warning: Light bulbs generate heat. This probably isn't a surprise to you, but it is something you need to take into consideration. The maximum allowable temperature for wood, paper, and textiles (the stuff of lamps and shades) is 194°F (90°C) as measured in an 86°F (30°C) room. All of the lamps in the book were designed to work with compact florescent bulbs, LEDs, or incandescent bulbs of 60 watts or less. If you stick with these, heat should not be an issue.

If you are concerned about heat build up, invest in an infrared digital thermometer (about $50 online). These instruments allow you to point them at a surface (most include a small laser for targeting) to get a readout of how hot it is. The area to target is the underside of the shade closest to the bulb as shown in the photo

A digital thermometer can give you an instant reading of the surface temperature of your lamp shade. Leave the lamp on for a good half hour before checking it. To allow a bit of a safety factor, change to a lower temperature bulb if the surface temperature exceeds 176°F.

Wiring LEDs

Working with LEDs is much like working with regular light bulbs except the wires are much smaller and the connections are made with solder and wire nuts rather than simply tightening a couple of screws. You still have two wires to deal with, and you still need to keep track of their polarity. If you use the same Hampton Bay LED

kits I used, you'll need to clip the connectors off the ends of both the leads that come from the puck and those that come from the transformer as shown in the photo, below left. After you feed the wire from the transformer into the lamp, tie a knot in the wire to keep it from pulling back out of the hole as shown in the photo, below right.

To make the connections between the LEDs, the transformer and the switch, start by splitting the wires into their separate con-

While your LED's may come with various plugs for connecting them together and to their transformer, you'll need to clip them off for use in the lamp designs in this book.

As you tie the wire to keep it from pulling out of the lamp, leave about 4" or so of wire to work with on the LED side of the knot.

ductors and stripping about ½" of insulation off each end. Take note of the insulation on the leads. The positive sides have very small printing on them while the negative sides have a series of dashes. Twist the positive wires together and solder them as shown in the photo, below. After the joint cools, cap it with a small wire nut. Fasten the two negative leads to either side of the SPST rocker switch (from Radio Shack) and solder as shown in the photo at right.

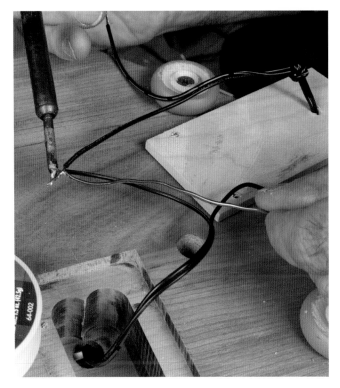

To solder two wires together, twist them first to make a good physical connection. Then apply heat to the bare metal with your soldering iron. Once the pieces seem hot enough (with a little practice, you'll know) touch the joint with the end of a length of resin core electrical solder (also a Radio Shack item). If things are hot enough, the solder will flow and coat the wires, locking them together. Don't try to melt the solder with the tip of the iron, the wires themselves have to be hot enough or the solder won't stick.

Soldering wires to a switch is essentially the same as soldering two wires together. Poke the wire through the hole in the switch terminal and twist it back on itself. Apply heat and solder to make the connection.

YOU AND THE UL

If you take a look at all the electrical components you're using for your lamp(s), you'll notice they each have a sticker somewhere on them saying they are UL-approved. The UL (Underwriter's Laboratory, Inc.) is an organization which oversees the manufacture of all things electrical in the USA. Think of them as a watchdog agency that keeps an eye on the safety of the various devices being sold.

It is good practice to use UL approved components in your lamps, but if you intend to sell your lamps,* you'll need to get UL approval for the lamps themselves. Registering with the

UL costs a couple thousand dollars up-front and then a few hundred dollars yearly to maintain your status along with the cost of the stickers. With this in mind, I have seen a number of handmade lamps for sale without UL approval. The trouble you will face is with liability should one of your lamps cause a fire.

*Keep in mind you are welcome to build the lamps in this book for your own use, or to give as gifts. If you want to market them however, you'll need to contact me to work out a licensing agreement.

THE **PROJECTS**

BUILDING LAMPS IS A FUN COMBINATION of woodworking and mechanical assembly. As far as the woodworking goes, the lamps presented here use a wide variety of techniques — pretty much everything you do to build furniture including shaping, joinery and finishing. And within each of these categories, you'll find a range of complexity. In shaping, for example, many of the lamps include moulded edges that are cut on a router table; a few of them rely on turned shapes created on the lathe; others have tapered parts; and a few even include bent wood. The joints run the gamut from basic dadoes and rabbets to compound miters, biscuits, and box joints. And the finishes range from those that can simply be wiped on and leave the wood with a "natural" appearance, to those that require a few more intermediate steps and add a stroke or two of color beyond the tans and browns typical to most furniture making.

On the mechanical side, you'll find a whole slew of products that have been developed specifically around making lamps. The challenge is how to wed these pieces to your woodwork. In designing these lamps, I've tried to make this blending of mechanical and wooden parts as simple and straightforward as possible. Many of the final bits of assembly are made with screws both to facilitate running wires and to allow for easy disassembly at some point in the future should repairs be in order.

One of the most exciting things I find about building lamps in my shop is that since they don't require a lot of material or time, I feel I can experiment and try things I would be reluctant to pursue on a larger, more complex project. As you page through the book thinking about which of the lamps to build, I encourage you to expand your woodworking horizons and try some techniques that seem challenging. Bend some wood if you haven't done so before; invest a little money in dye and spread a little color around. Build these lamps as presented, or modify them to suit your needs and abilities. When you get finished, shoot a picture or two and send them my way. I'd love to see what you've accomplished.

DESPITE THEIR VERY DIFFERENT APPEARANCES, THESE THREE LAMPS ARE VERY SIMILAR IN THE WAY THEY ARE MADE.
WALNUT, CHERRY AND WENGE AND WHITE OAK

(1) **SLAB** LAMPS

USING A SINGLE PIECE OF WOOD FOR A LAMP BASE is a great way to show off a choice piece with spectacular grain. Or it can be a neat opportunity to simply play with shapes and forms. These particular lamps came from a series of doodles I drew on the back of one of my many to-do lists.

Each lamp in this group makes use of a relatively short length of thick (8/4-10/4) stock. While each of the lamps has a different look to it, the basic process is the same: Drill or rout a hole for the cord, dado for the feet, cut out the shape, refine the shape, assemble. I've included drawings so you can reproduce each of the designs shown here, but don't feel limited by this. Start doodling on your own, or go through your bin of offcuts and let the wood be your guide. You'll be amazed at the shapes you can come up with simply by looking at knots and other grain patterns.

One thing to keep in mind, you'll end up with better lamps if you think of ways to modify the shape after you cut it out. I often refer to these as "cookie cutter" lamps, but you'll probably want to go beyond a cut-out shape with routed edges. One of my college professors talked about taking material "out of stock." What he meant was changing the material beyond the way it comes from a machine. Tapering, doing some hand shaping, or even drilling holes in a shape can keep it from looking like it was simply stamped out.

INCHES (MILLIMETERS)

REFERENCE	QUANTITY	PART	STOCK	THICKNESS	(mm)	WIDTH	(mm)	LENGTH	(mm)
Triangle Lamp									
A	1	body	cherry	2	(51)	$7^5/_8$	(194)	16	(406)
B	2	feet	wenge	1	(25)	$1^1/_8$	(29)	$5^3/_8$	(137)
C	1	top	wenge	$9/_{16}$	(14)	$1^3/_4$	(45)	4	(102)

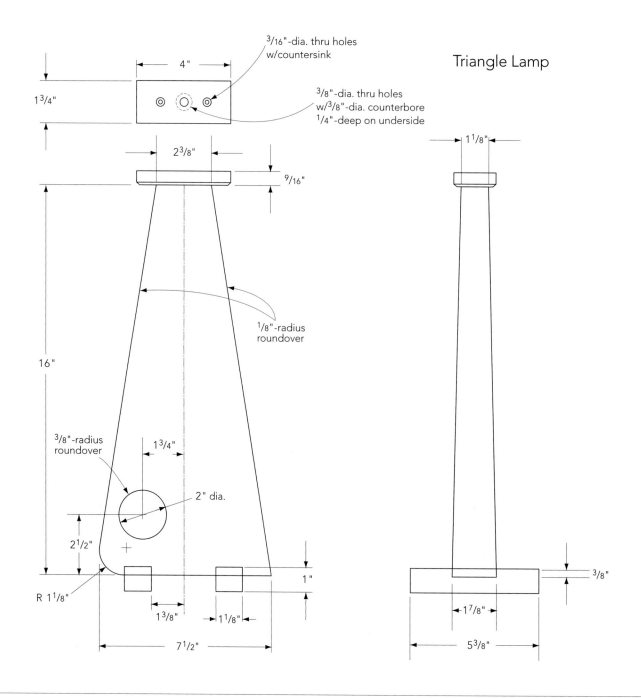

$3/_{16}$"-dia. thru holes
w/countersink

$3/_8$"-dia. thru holes
w/$3/_8$"-dia. counterbore
$1/_4$"-deep on underside

Triangle Lamp

4 "

$1^3/_4$"

$2^3/_8$"

$9/_{16}$"

$1^1/_8$"

$1/_8$"-radius
roundover

16 "

$3/_8$"-radius
roundover

$1^3/_4$"

2 " dia.

$2^1/_2$"

1 "

R $1^1/_8$"

$1^3/_8$"

$1^1/_8$"

$7^1/_2$"

$3/_8$"

$1^7/_8$"

$5^3/_8$"

INCHES (MILLIMETERS)

REFERENCE	QUANTITY	PART	STOCK	THICKNESS	(mm)	WIDTH	(mm)	LENGTH	(mm)
Oval Lamp									
A	1	body	white oak	2	(51)	9¼	(235)	14	(356)
B	1	foot	white oak	1¼	(32)	1¾	(45)	8	(203)
C	1	top	white oak	9/16	(14)	2¼	(57)	6	(152)

HARDWARE (for each lamp)

Lamp Socket w/ Switch
1/8 IP x 1¼" Lamp Nipple with
  2 1/8 IP Hex Nuts
Lamp Wings (for holding harp)
Lamp Cord
2" Screws for holding Feet (2)
1½" Screws for holding top (2)
Lamp Shade

Oval Lamp

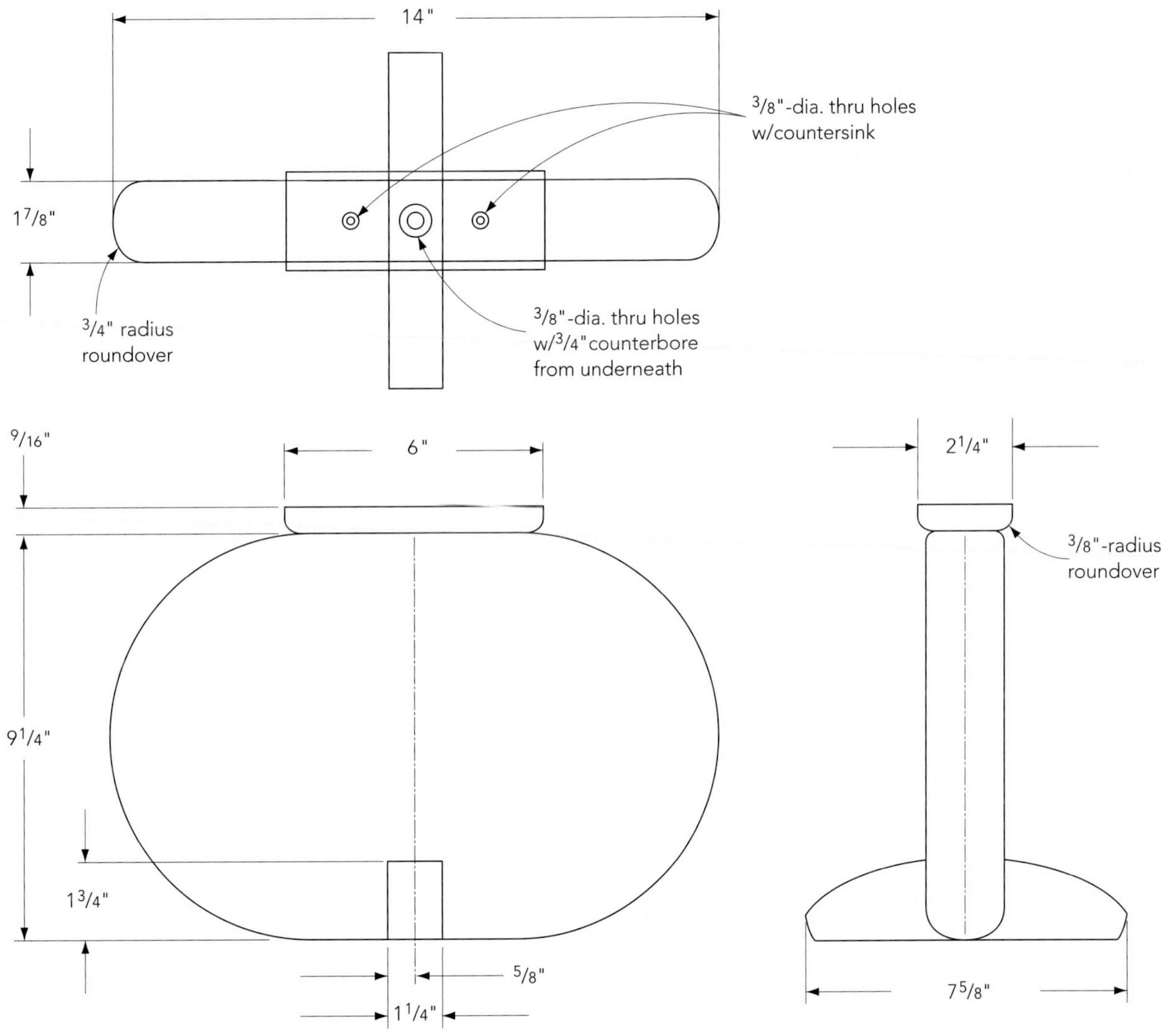

14"

1⁷/₈"

3/8"-dia. thru holes
w/countersink

3/4" radius
roundover

3/8"-dia. thru holes
w/3/4"counterbore
from underneath

9/16"

6"

9¼"

1¾"

5/8"

1¼"

2¼"

3/8"-radius
roundover

7⁵/₈"

INCHES (MILLIMETERS)

REFERENCE	QUANTITY	PART	STOCK	THICKNESS	(mm)	WIDTH	(mm)	LENGTH	(mm)
Vase-shaped Lamp									
A	1	body	walnut	2¼	(57)	8½	(216)	11	(279)
B	1	foot	walnut	1³⁄₈	(35)	1³⁄₈	(35)	6½	(165)
C	1	top	walnut	⁹⁄₁₆	(14)	2½	(64)	5	(127)

Vase-Shaped Lamp

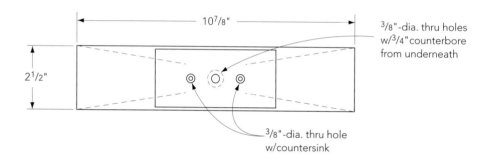

10⁷⁄₈"

2½"

³⁄₈"-dia. thru holes
w/³⁄₄"counterbore
from underneath

³⁄₈"-dia. thru hole
w/countersink

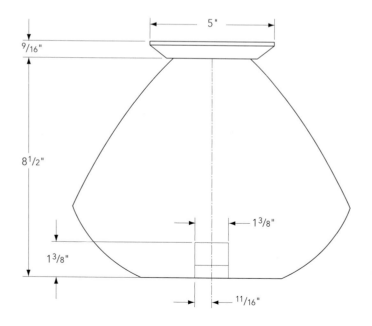

5"

⁹⁄₁₆"

8½"

1³⁄₈"

1³⁄₈"

11⁄₁₆"

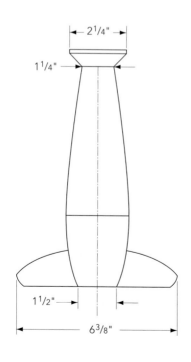

2¼"

1¼"

1½"

6³⁄₈"

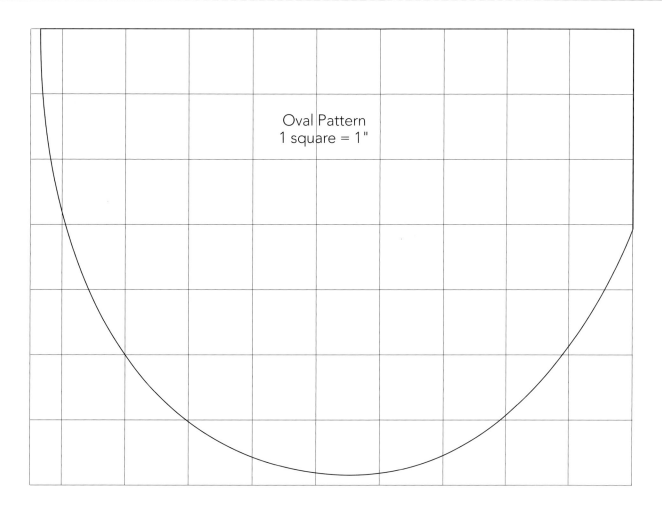

Oval Pattern
1 square = 1"

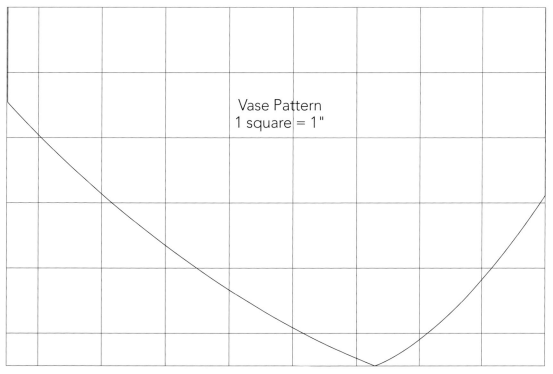

Vase Pattern
1 square = 1"

Fabrication

Prepare your stock by starting with a piece of thick material. I looked for stock that was wide enough to get the shapes I wanted without having to glue pieces together, but there is no reason you couldn't edge glue narrow pieces to make up the piece you need. Cut the piece roughly to length. Then joint and plane it to make it flat and smooth, if necessary.

Lay out the shape by drawing a vertical center line down the middle of your piece. You'll be using this as a reference throughout the construction process. By vertical, I mean a centerline that runs up and down when the lamp is in use.

To lay out the shape of the triangular lamp, I simply measured equal distances on ether side of the centerline at the top and bottom and connected the dots with a straightedge. For the other two designs, I made up patterns as shown in Photo 1.

ONE When your shape involves curves, there is nothing like a pattern to make layout easier. And, because these lamps are symmetrical, you only need a half pattern. I make patterns from ¼" plywood or MDF. Make the layout by enlarging the drawing. Then cut and sand it to shape. Hold the pattern on the centerline to lay out the curves on your work piece.

TWO If the grain in your lamp runs from side to side (horizontally), You can drill the hole on a drill press. Extend the center line across the top and bottom of the piece and drill the hole from either end with a ½" bit. If your drill press has a limited travel (mine only goes 3") drill as far as you can and stop the machine. Raise the table with the bit in the hole, then start and drill to the limit of the bit's length. Turn the piece over and drill the rest of the hole from the other end.

THREE For lamps where the grain runs up and down (vertically), it is better to rout the hole rather than trying to drill into endgrain. Cut the piece in half (right on the center line) on the table saw. Rout each half on a router table with a ½" core box bit. Glue the two halves back together. To keep any squeeze-out from blocking the hole, apply a little paste wax to the routed surfaces prior to glue up. After the glue dries, you can run a length of dowel through the hole to open it up — the beads of glue inside will simply pop off.

FOUR A stationary belt sander is the ideal tool for cleaning up curves. I keep a course (50 grit) belt on mine. I find the course grit removes material quickly without building up too much heat. With a finer grit, I find the heat can build up so much it can cause the piece I'm sanding to develop small checks. Make sure the table is square to the platen behind the belt before sanding.

One of the key things in designing and making lamps is allowing access for the wire that powers the light. In these designs, the wire runs up through a hole drilled (or routed) through the center of the workpiece. It is much easier to put this hole through before you cut the workpiece to shape. How you do this depends on how the grain is oriented in your lamp as shown in Photos 2 and 3.

Set up a dado head and cut the dados for the feet. Again, this step is much easier to accomplish before you cut the pieces to their final shape. The exact width of the dado blade isn't important because the cuts you are making are wider than most standard dado blades can make in a single pass. Hold your piece vertically against the miter gauge and make the cut(s) in several passes.

Finally, you're ready to cut the pieces to shape. Cut along the lines with a band saw. Sand the curves to refine their shape as shown in Photo 4. I cut the angled sides of the triangular lamp on the band saw and then ran the piece across the jointer to smooth away the saw marks. For the curved corner, I traced a tuna can then cut and sanded

the curve. I also drilled the big hole through the piece before moving on to the next step.

In addition to being sawn to shape, two of these lamps are also tapered in thickness. The triangle lamp tapers from bottom to top, while the vase-shaped lamp tapers from the middle to the top and to the bottom. Making the taper on the triangle lamp is a job for the jointer as show in Photo 5. The other tapers are done with a hand plane as shown in Photo 6.

FIVE A jointer does a great job of tapering. To get set up, set the depth of cut to 1/16". With the power off, position your workpiece so about 1/4" of its leading edge is resting on the outfeed table. Clamp a stop block to the infeed table at the end of the trailing edge. To make the cut, hold the workpiece above the cutter head with its trailing edge against the stop block. Carefully pivot the guard out of the way and lower the workpiece to the table. This sounds scarier than it is. Continue, counting the number of passes you make until the board has the desired taper. Repeat the process for the other side making the same number of passes. Remove the stop block and reset the depth of cut to about 1/32". Give each side a final pass to clean up any irregularities.

SIX Make the curved taper on the vase-shaped lamp by planing the piece with a hand plane. Draw marks on the top and bottom so you can see when to stop.

7

SEVEN Shape the edges of the oval lamp with a ¾" radius roundover bit. Use a ½" radius roundover bit for the outside edges of the triangle lamp, and a ⅜" radius roundover bit for the inside of the hole.

Round over the edges of both the triangle and oval lamps on the router table as shown in Photo 7. The edges of the vase-shaped lamp stay square and are just broken with sandpaper.

Cut the feet to the sizes listed. The feet for the triangle lamp stay rectangular, but those for the other two lamps are curved. Bandsaw and sand them to shape. Drill and countersink screw holes to attach the feet to the lamps. Also drill the feet for the oval and vase-shaped lamps in the center for the cord.

Cut the top to the size listed. Bore a ¹³⁄₃₂" hole through the center of the piece to accept the lamp nipple. Counter bore the hole from the bottom side of the piece for the nipple's nut. Also bore and countersink screw holes on either side of the center hole. Shape the bottom edges on the router table. For the oval lamp, use a ½" roundover bit. For the other two, a 45° chamfer bit.

ASSEMBLY & INSTALLATION

1. Sand all the parts and finish them with your favorite wood finish. It is a lot easier to finish the pieces before you screw everything together. The lamps in the photos were finished with several coats of Minwax Antique Oil Finish.
2. When the finish is dry, slide the nipple through the hole in the top and lock it in place with a nut on either side. Be sure to capture the wings for the lamp's harp under the nut on the upper surface of the top.
3. Screw the top and the foot (feet) to the lamp body.
4. Finish wiring the lamp as described starting on page 8.

WHILE THE BASES AND LIGHT FIXTURES ARE QUITE DIFFERENT IN APPEARANCE, BOTH OF THESE LAMPS ARE CONSTRUCTED IN A VERY SIMILAR MANNER. **CONICAL BASE: CHERRY AND ASH HEMISPHERICAL BASE: WALNUT AND ASH.**

2 BENTWOOD LAMPS

I FIRST SKETCHED THIS LAMP several years ago and have toyed with the design ever since, looking for a good excuse to actually make it. I say lamp, because the original idea was just a for a single lamp. But as I began developing the ideas for this book, that original sketch morphed into two similar, yet distinct designs.

The hardest part of the development process was coming up with the actual lighting part for both lamps. I originally had in mind using a fixture from Ikea — a conical metal shade with a wire and switch that was ready to hang. I already had a couple of these and they looked pretty good. But when I started sourcing things, I found they were no longer available. Go figure. By that time, I had both lamps just about ready for their electrics. What to do?

I put both lamps on the back burner while contemplating the options. Eventually I took both with me as I made the rounds of the various local lamp supply houses and home centers. I opened a lot of boxes and talked to a number of salespeople before arriving at the lamps you see here. I like the way the fixtures look, and also like that the parts should be readily available at a well-stocked home center.

If you opt to make the hemispherical design, you have simply to purchase a pendant lamp. It is a little on the pricey side, but very straightforward to install. For the conical design, you'll need an 8" globe, less money, but you'll need to spend a little more time and effort making a mount for it.

From a woodworking point of view, the techniques involved here are woodturning and wood bending. The bases are both turned, meaning you'll need access to a lathe. The shapes are quite straightforward to make, so even if you don't have a lot to turning experience, they shouldn't be hard to do.

More challenging is the bent piece. It is made using a technique called bent lamination. To accomplish this, you'll cut your stock into thin, flexible strips and then glue these strips back together as they are clamped around a curved form. The technique produces strong, consistent bends without the use of steam. It can seem a little intimidating at first, but once you have tried it, you'll soon be making all sorts of bent shapes.

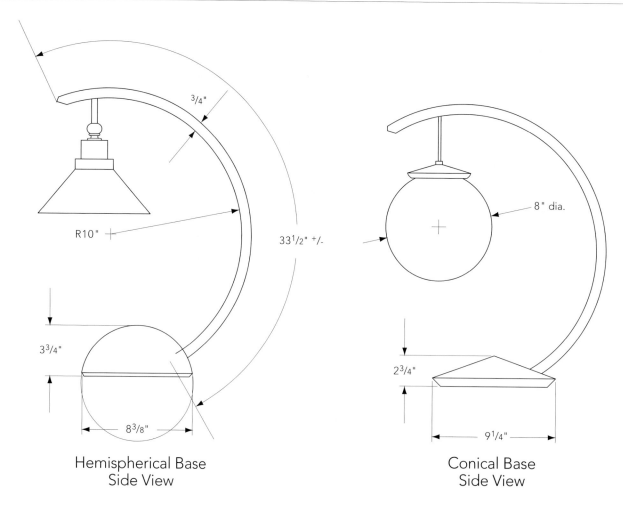

Hemispherical Base
Side View

Conical Base
Side View

Fabrication

Make the form for your bent piece by gluing and screwing together two pieces of ¾" MDF, plywood, or particle board. Draw a 20" diameter circle on the top piece and keep your screws well away from this line. Cut the circle out on the band saw, keeping outside the line. Then use a ½" straight bit in a router to cut the form to a perfect circle as shown in Photo 1.

ONE Attach your router to a trammel jig to help you cut a perfectly circular form. Plans for the jig in the photo are shown in Router Trammel on page 30.

INCHES (MILLIMETERS)

REFERENCE	QUANTITY	PART	STOCK	THICKNESS	(mm)	WIDTH	(mm)	LENGTH	(mm)	COMMENTS
A	11	strips	ash	$3/32$	(2.5)	$1^3/8$	(35)	42	(1067)	
B	1	hemispherical base	walnut	$3^3/4$	(95)	$8^3/8$	(213)			
C	1	conical base	cherry	$2^3/4$	(70)	$9^1/4$	(235)			
D	1	cap	cherry	1	(25)	$4^3/4$	(121)			
E	1	cover plate	cherry	$1/8$	(3)	$2^3/4$	(70)			

HARDWARE

Hemispherical Base

Pendent Lamp (Hampton Bay #462 537)
Lamp Cord w/Line Switch
Wire Nuts (2)
Feet (3) (Woodcraft #50S41)

Conical Base

Lamp Cord w/Line Switch
$1/8$ IP Bracket Cap
$1/8$ IP Hex Nut

$1/8$ IP x $1^3/4$" Nipple
Lamp Socket
Feet (3) (Woodcraft #50S41)

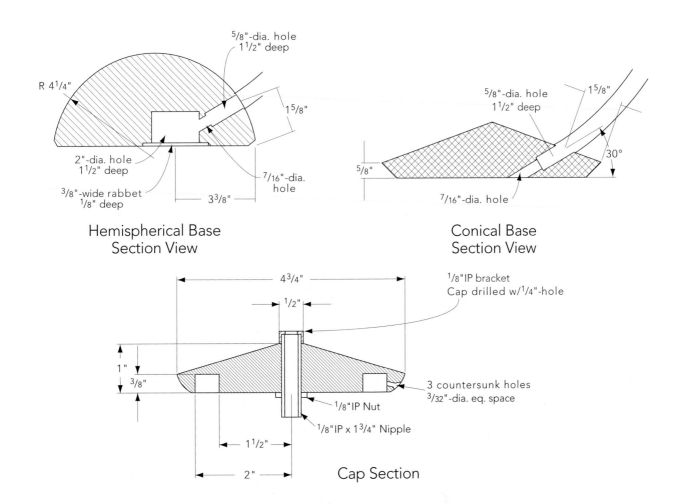

Hemispherical Base
Section View

Conical Base
Section View

Cap Section

ROUTER TRAMMEL

This trammel jig will allow you to cut circles 2" to 30" in diameter. It is designed to be screwed to the base of a hand-held router. I prefer a plunge router as it allows me to start a circular cut with the bit out-of-contact from the workpiece. I made my trammel from a scrap of Baltic birch plywood with a hardwood slider. The pivot is a 5/16" bolt cut to fit. The slider fits in a T-groove cut in the underside of the jig. It is locked in place by tightening the knob. The knob is threaded through a T-nut and presses on a metal disc, which presses on the slider. I used a slug from an electric junction box for the metal plate, but a quarter would also work well.

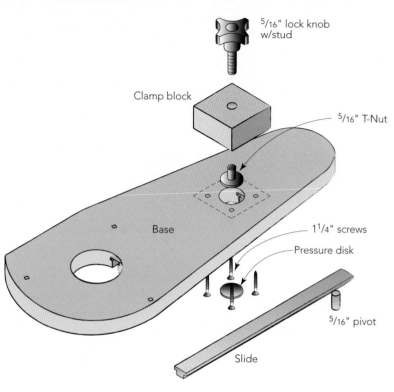

5/16" lock knob w/stud

Clamp block

5/16" T-Nut

Base

1 1/4" screws

Pressure disk

5/16" pivot

Slide

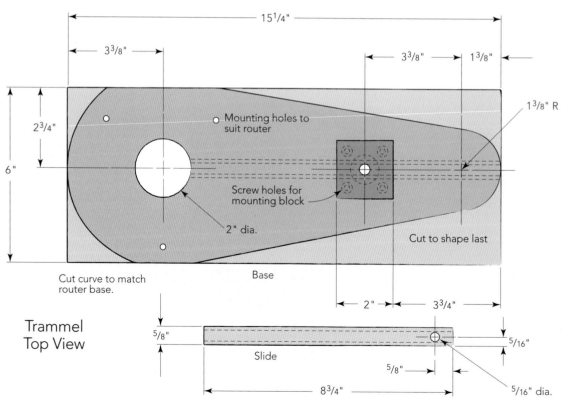

15 1/4"

3 3/8"

3 3/8"

1 3/8"

2 3/4"

1 3/8" R

6 "

Mounting holes to suit router

Screw holes for mounting block

2" dia.

Cut to shape last

Cut curve to match router base.

Base

Trammel
Top View

5/8"

2 "

3 3/4"

Slide

5/16"

5/8"

5/16" dia.

8 3/4"

Cut a piece of 6/4 stock so it is 42" long. Joint and plane it, leaving it as thick as possible — you'll cut the bent pieces to width later. Also joint one edge so it is straight and rip the other edge to make it parallel. Rip a series of strips off the edge of the board for bending as shown in Photo 2. Rather than trying to set the fence for such a narrow cut, I set up a stop block to the left of the blade to easily move and set the fence for the next strip. I used ash for bends on my lamps. Ash bends very well (as does oak). Even so, I had to cut the strips just 3⁄32" thick so I could get them around the relatively tight curve. Make a test cut from the material you are using and bend it around your form to see if you have the thickness right.

To set the stop (I use the butt end of a feather board), use the rip fence to position the board so the offcut is the thickness you are after. Adjust the stop so it just kisses the left side of the board an inch or two in front of the blade and lock it in place. Make the first cut. Then adjust the rip fence so the left side of the board just kisses the stop. Make the second cut. Keep going, adjusting the fence after each cut until you have enough strips. For each of the lamps, you'll need nine strips, plus a couple extras to help distribute the clamp pressure.

Apply glue to strips one, two, three and four and strips six, seven and eight. Stack all nine strips in order and place them against the form. Leaving strip five without glue means your bent piece will initially come off the form in two pieces. This will allow you to rout a groove for the cord before making the final glue up. Add the two extra strips (without glue) to the stack to help distribute the clamping pressure. Wrap a band clamp around the strips and the form, and tighten it to wrap the strip around the form as shown in Photo 3.

Once you have the band clamp tight, add a couple clamps to help pull the ends in as shown in Photo 4 on the next page. Allow the glue to dry for at least 24 hours.

While the glue is drying, cut a chunk of stock for the base. For the conical lamp, I used a piece of 12/4 cherry and for the hemispherical lamp, a piece of 16/4 walnut. If you can't find such thick material, you can face glue two or more thinner pieces together to make up the necessary thickness.

TWO When cutting strips for bent lamination, keeping the pieces in the order they were cut allows you to glue them up so the grain matches. To help keep things straight, draw a series of diagonal lines across the board so you can put them back in order should things get mixed up.

THREE Apply glue and use a band clamp to wrap the strips around the form. I fastened a C-clamp to my bench and used it as a fulcrum to help get the pieces bent into shape.

TIP Cover the curved surfaces of your bending forms with a layer of plastic packing tape to help prevent gluing the bent piece right to the form. If you can find it, the best glue for bent lamination is plastic resin glue. This powdered adhesive is mixed with water to a medium viscosity. When it sets, it forms a very rigid bond. While it works, aliphatic resin (yellow) glue has a tendency to slip slightly under load (applied by the strips trying to straighten themselves even after the glue has set). This can leave the ends of your bent pieces feeling slightly stepped over time.

FOUR Using a band clamp on a bent lamination gives nice even pressure, but may not be quite enough to draw the very ends in. Adding a metal clamp at either end ensures the ends as well as the middle part of the bend will conform to the form.

FIVE & SIX Turn the blank round first, then turn it to its final shape. You'll probably get a smoother cut if you start at the center and work towards the outside edge.

Cut the piece round, screw a face plate to it, and mount it on your lathe as shown in Photos 5 & 6. Turn the piece to shape. If you are making the hemispherical base, lightly mark the center point after sanding the piece. (The center of the conical base will be evident)

Once the base is turned to shape, remove it from the lathe but leave the face plate screwed to the bottom. Tip the table on your drill press over so it is about 30° from vertical. You can check this quickly by chucking a ½" bit and measuring the angle between it and the table with a 30-60 drafting triangle.

Mark a radius line on the base that runs with the grain. On the hemispherical base, you'll need a flexible straightedge to draw along. A radius line is simply any line that runs from the edge through the center point. Mark the line 1⅝" up from the edge to indicate the location of the hole for the bent piece.

Use a handscrew to grip the face plate and a C-clamp to hold the handscrew to the drill press table as shown in Photo 7. Chuck a ⅝" forstner bit in the drill press and align it with the mark you made on the radius line. Also check to make sure the bit is in line with the radius line. Drill the hole, making it about 1¼" deep. Note: In the photo, I used a ¾" bit and found it made too big a hole in relationship to the size of the bent piece. Were I to remake this lamp, I would definitely use the smaller, ⅝" bit.

Remove the face plate from the underside of the base. Place the base on a piece of scrap and continue the hole with a ⁷⁄₁₆" bit in a hand drill to create a passage for the wire. The exact angle of this hole isn't critical.

Allow the bent pieces to dry for at least 24 hours before removing the clamps. They will probably spring back away from the form somewhat. Don't worry about this, it happens frequently when making bent laminations. At this point, you should have two bent pieces, the inner one slightly thicker than the outer one. Scrape away as much of the glue squeeze-out as possible.

Joint one edge of each of the bent pieces to make the edge straight and square as shown in Photos 8a and 8b. This is why it is best to leave the laminations as wide as possible to begin with. With so many individual pieces being

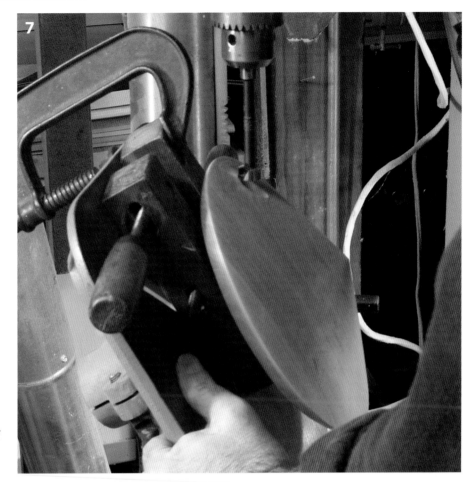

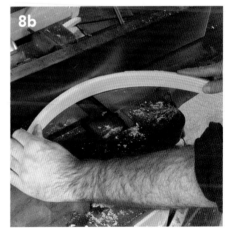

SEVEN Even with a forstner bit, drilling the angled hole in the base isn't easy. Because the bit grabs on one side first, it will have a tendency to deflect somewhat towards the upper part of the base. The hole placement isn't so critical that this will be an issue. However, don't back the bit all the way out of the hole until you have finished drilling. I made this mistake, and when I went to start drilling again, the bit made the hole somewhat oblong.

EIGHT Jointing a bent piece is little different from jointing a straight piece. Keep the face of the piece tight against the fence and pivot the piece through the cut, maintaining contact with both the infeed and the outfeed tables. The radius of these bends was tight enough that I removed the guard from my jointer. Be extra alert as you cut and keep your fingers well away from the cutter head.

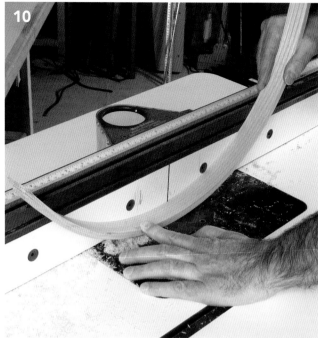

glued up at the same time, it is quite easy for something to slip out of alignment in the process. Having a little extra material to deal with gives you a slight margin for error.

To make the second sides of the bent pieces parallel to the sides you just jointed, set the table saw fence to cut the pieces as wide as possible, while still cutting away all the irregularities. Keep the blade as low as possible and roll the bent pieces through the cut as shown in Photo 9.

Rout a ⁵⁄₁₆"-wide × ¼"-deep groove for the cord down the middle of the inner bend with a straight bit in a table-mounted router. Again, you'll need to roll the piece through the cut as shown in Photo 10. Try to keep the piece in contact with the table right where the bit is.

After cutting the groove, glue the two bent pieces together using a band clamp and the bending form as you did before. Just apply glue to the inner piece. You don't want so much glue on things that the squeeze-out plugs up the groove. Again, allow things to dry for at least 24 hours before removing the clamp(s). Scrape away any squeeze-out before jointing one edge. Rip the opposite side to clean it up. Then measure the width of the piece and check to see how well centered the groove is. Cut the piece to its final width, removing any excess from both sides to keep the groove centered.

NINE Ripping a bent piece is only slightly more difficult than ripping a flat one. As you cut, roll the piece so the section being cut is in contact with the table at the front of the blade. Keep a push stick handy to push the last few inches of the cut past the blade.

TEN Routing a groove in a bent piece is very similar to ripping the piece — you have to roll it through the cut. Make the groove in two passes, raising the bit in-between.

ELEVEN Crosscut bent pieces as you would straight ones — hold the concave side of the piece firmly against the miter gauge and push it through the cut. When I made this cut, having the angle set to a specific degree seemed important. But after going through the next few steps I realized it would have been easier to cut the piece off square (or as square as you can cut a bent piece). So save yourself some trouble and cut your piece off square — you'll probably still have to angle the miter gauge somewhat.

Use the miter gauge on your saw to cut one end of the of the bent piece as shown in Photo 11.

Make a round tenon on the end of the piece you just cut. I used a chisel to establish the shoulder line and then rounded the piece with a file as shown in Photo 12. Once you have the piece fit into the hole, you can fine tune the fit of the shoulder.

If you are using a round globe for the light fixture, you'll need to turn a cap to hold the globe itself and to serve as a base for the light socket. Surface a piece of 6/4 material so you have two flat sides. Cut a 5"-diameter disk on the band saw.

Mount the blank on a faceplate, taking care to center it well. Turn a ½"-wide × ½"-deep groove to accommodate the rim of the globe. Have the globe on hand so you can check the fit.

Remove the piece and remount it with the grooved side against the faceplate. Centering the piece this time is even more important. Turn the lid to a conical profile as shown in the Cap Section on page 29. Mark the center with an awl.

Remove the cap from the lathe and drill a $^{13}/_{32}$" hole through its center.

Locate three points spread equally around the edge of the lid and mark them for the holes for the screws that will hold the globe in place as shown in the Cap Section. Drill these holes with a $^{3}/_{32}$" bit then countersink them as shown in Photo 13.

Place the bent piece in the hole and hold the light fixture in place to determine its exact location. When you are happy with where you think the light should hang, mark its location on the underside of the bent piece. Drill a $^{5}/_{16}$" hole that intersects with the cord groove at this location.

Round over all four edges of the bent piece with a $^{3}/_{16}$" radius roundover bit chucked in a table-mounted router.

Cut off the bent piece at a point somewhat beyond the hole you just drilled. For the conical-based lamp, I allowed the piece to extend about 3½". For the hemispherical-based lamp, I think a 2" extension looks better. Cut a rectangle of scrap to fit in the cord groove and glue it in place. Shape and sand the cut end so it terminates neatly.

For the hemispherical-based lamp, drill a 2" diameter hole in the underside of the base centered on the $^{7}/_{16}$" hole you

TWELVE File the end of the bent piece into a round tenon that fits snugly in the hole you drilled in the base. Take care to keep the cord groove centered as best you can in the tenon (it will be slightly off to one side). The really important thing is not to file into the side of the groove.

THIRTEEN Install three #4 x $^{3}/_{8}$" screws equally-spaced around the edge of the lid to hold the globe in place.

TIP When mounting small pieces on a faceplate, I frequently use double-sided carpet tape. I cover the faceplate with tape and then squeeze it to my blank with a clamp to "set" the adhesive. In better than thirty years of turning, I have yet to have the tape fail. In fact, the difficult part is often trying to pry the piece loose after I'm done with the lathe.

drilled earlier for the cord. Make this hole about 2" deep. To hold the base as I drilled, I used a piece of the Styrofoam packaging that came with the light fixture. It had a circular cutout in one side that cradled the base perfectly. Cut a ⅜"-wide × ⅛"-deep rabbet around this hole with a rabbeting bit chucked in a table-mounted router as shown in Photo 14. Cut a ⅛"-thick disk that fits in the rabbet to form a cover for the hole. Drill a ¼" hole in the center of the disk for the cord to escape.

Glue the bent piece in the hole in the base. Check to make sure it is plumb when viewed from the front. Drill an ⅛"-diameter hole in the bottom of the base up into the bent piece for a dowel to re-inforce the joint. Be sure not to use too long a dowel, or you'll block the cord groove.

Attach three feet to the underside of the base, spacing them equally near the edge. I call them feet, but they are really wooden

FOURTEEN Because the lighting fixture I used for the hemispherical-based lamp was meant to be hardwired, I had to make a space in the base for it to be connected to a regular lamp cord. Drilling a 2" diameter hole and then fitting it with a cover plate handles the connection beautifully. A couple screws hold the cover in place, yet allow access for repairs if necessary.

wheels. Countersink the axle holes a little so the screws won't scratch the surface where you place your lamp.

Finish the wooden parts with your favorite wood finish. As with most of the pieces in this book, I finished these lamps with several coats of Minwax Antique Oil Finish, a wiping varnish. As a final touch, glue felt disks to the bottoms of the feet.

ASSEMBLY HEMISPHERICAL AND CONICAL BASE

Hemispherical Base

1. The pendent light comes with a wire attached. Strip away the outer insulation from most of this wire, leaving about 5" of it right at the fixture. You will now have three individual wires — one black, one white, and a colored one (probably green or blue). The black and white ones are the actual conductors, the colored one is the ground. Feed all three up through the hole in the bent piece and work them around to the big hole in the base.

2. Pull on the three wires, drawing the fixture up to the bent piece. You may need to cut away a little more of the outer insulation to get the fixture to hang where you want it. Drive a screw into the bottom of the hole in the base and wrap the colored ground wire around it to serve as an anchor for the fixture. Lamp cords don't usually have a ground wire, so you can cut off any excess.

3. Feed the end of the lamp cord up through the hole in the cover plate. Make sure the outside of the cover is toward the plug end of the cord. Tie an overhand knot in the cord so it cannot pull back through the hole. Leave about 4" of wire beyond the knot to make the connections. Split the wire into two separate leads and strip about ½" of insulation off of each.

4. Cut the black and white wires from the fixture so you have about 6" of wire for the connections. Strip about ½" of insulation off each of these wires, too.

5. Connect the white wire to the ribbed wire from the lamp cord and the black to the other wire. Twist the connections tightly and cap with wire nuts. Make sure the nuts cover all exposed metal.

6. Tuck the wires into the hole and screw the cover plate in place.

Conical Base

1. Feed the lamp wire up through the base into the bent piece. Keep pushing it until you reach the hole at the top. At this point, you may need to pull the end with needle nose pliers to get it down through the hole. Pull about 12" of wire through to give yourself some extra to work with.

2. Drill a ¼" hole through the center of the bracket cap. I held the cap with a chuck on my lathe and drilled it, holding the bit in a second chuck in the tailstock. If you aren't set up to do it this way, you can wrap the cap with a few turns of masking tape, then grab it with a set of vise grips and drill it on your drill press.

3. Thread the bracket cap onto the nipple and push the nipple down through the hole in the cap. Thread the nut onto the nipple to hold it in place. Thread the base of the socket onto the nipple.

4. Feed the wire down through the nipple until about 6" of it extends out. Split the wire into two separate leads and tie them together so they can't pull back out. Strip about ½" of insulation from each end and make the connections to the socket. You may need to cut the leads shorter so everything fits. Be sure to connect the ribbed lead to the silver terminal and the other to the gold.

5. Put the socket together. Pull the wire back through the bent piece so the cap/socket assembly hangs where you want it to. There should be enough friction to keep it in place. If not, cut a wedge to fit into the hole in the base so you can tap it in to keep the wire from moving.

6. Add a bulb and the glass globe to finish things off.

Refer to the electrical section on page 8 for more information regarding the specifics of the electrical connections. If you aren't sure how to do the wiring consult with a licensed professional.

MY DESIGN INFLUENCES COME FROM ALL SORTS OF PLACES. THIS PARTICULAR LAMP HAS IT'S ROOTS IN 18TH CENTURY FURNITURE (THINK: HIGHBOY), ARCHITECTURE, AND EVEN MY SOCK DRAWER. REGARDLESS OF WHERE IT STARTED, I THINK THE LAMP HAS A FRESH, FUN LOOK TO IT THAT MAY ADD A SENSE OF WHIMSY TO A ROOM. **JATOBA, QUARTERSAWN SYCAMORE.**

③ **HARLEQUIN** LAMP

ROAMING THE AISLES of one of those big home centers, you never know what you're going to find. I started out with a vague idea that glass blocks might be useful in making lamps. What I didn't realize was how many different shapes, sizes, and textures they came in. I'll be returning to that part of the store soon, because I have plenty of other ideas to try out.

Among other blocks, I purchased a 4 x 8 x 4 block (essentially a half block) with the thought I could incorporate it into some kind of table lamp/nightlight. After a number of sketches, I came up with this design that incorporates an LED "puck" light into the base, and a regular light fixture above.

The face of the "box" under the glass block seemed to cry out for some kind of graphic treatment. The harlequin pattern is one I've played with a lot in the past few years — perhaps inspired by my argyle socks. (I have yet to acquire a sweater vest.)

Construction is straightforward, though the connections between the pieces rely on a biscuit joiner. If you don't have one of these tools in your shop, you could easily substitute dowels instead.

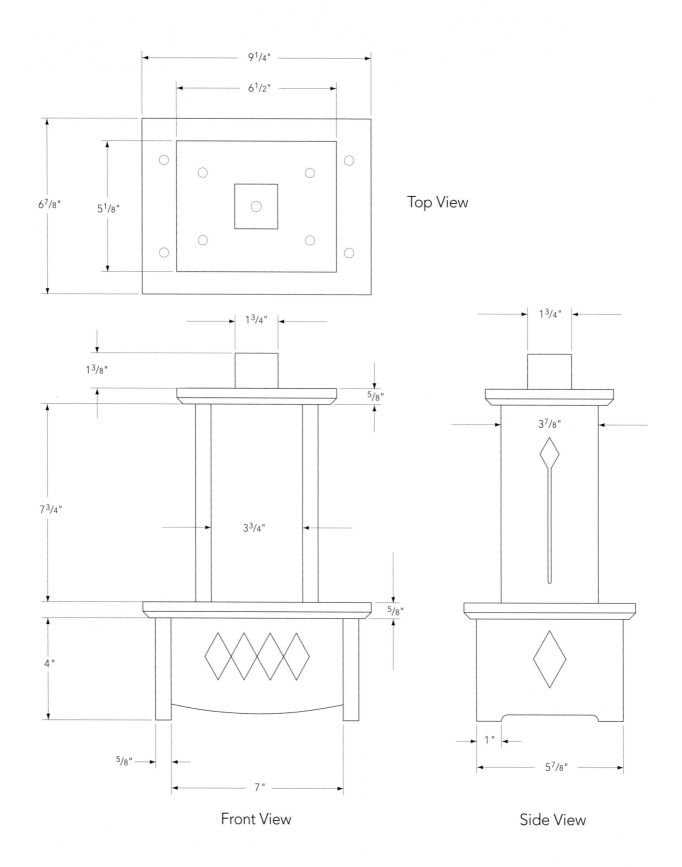

Top View

Front View

Side View

INCHES (MILLIMETERS)

REFERENCE	QUANTITY	PART	STOCK	THICKNESS	(mm)	WIDTH	(mm)	LENGTH	(mm)
A	1	top	jatoba	$5/8$	(16)	$5^1/8$	(130)	$6^1/2$	(165)
B	1	base	jatoba	$5/8$	(16)	$6^7/8$	(174)	$9^1/4$	(235)
C	1	puck support	jatoba	$5/8$	(16)	$3^3/4$	(95)	4	(102)
D	2	sides	jatoba	$5/8$	(16)	$3^7/8$	(98)	$7^3/4$	(197)
E	2	legs	jatoba	$5/8$	(16)	$5^7/8$	(149)	4	(102)
F	2	panels	sycamore	$3/8$	(10)	$3^3/4$	(95)	$7^1/2$	(191)
G	1	riser	jatoba	$1^3/8$	(35)	$1^3/4$	(45)	$1^3/4$	(45)
H	2	spacers	jatoba	$1/4$	(6)	$1^1/4$	(32)	$7^3/4$	(197)
J	1	bottom	plywood	$1/8$	(3)	$4^3/4$	(121)	7	(178)

HARDWARE

4 x 8 x 4 Glass Block
#8 x 1" Wood Screws (4)
#8 x $1^1/4$" Wood Screws (2)
#8 x 2" Wood Screws (12)
#6 x 1" Wood Screws (4)
LED Puck Kit
   (Hampton Bay #957 245)
SPST Rocker Switch
   (Radio Shack #275-690)
$1/8$ IP x $2^1/2$" Nipple
$1/8$ IP Hex Nuts (2)
Lamp Socket w/ Switch
Lamp Cord

Fabrication

Cut the top, bottom, sides, puck support, and legs to the sizes given in the Materials List. Draw a center line from front to back across the base. Center the glass block on this line and mark its sides as shown in Photo 1.

Cut slots for biscuits to join the sides to the top and base. Transfer the layout marks you made on the base to the underside of the top to maintain consistent spacing. Clamp the mating pieces together as shown in Photo 2 to align them for cutting. Also cut the slots for the biscuits that join the legs to the underside of the base. Mark the pieces so you know where they go, and which side is out.

Drill a 3" diameter hole through the center of the base for the puck lamp. Also drill a 3" diameter hole $1/4$" deep in the center of the puck support.

ONE Use the width of the glass block to determine the spacing of the side pieces. If in doubt, it is better to have the sides slightly too far apart than slightly too close together.

TWO Cut mating slots for a single biscuit in each of the joints connecting the sides to the base and the top as well as those connecting the legs to the base. Center the slots across the width of the pieces.

Chuck a 1" straight bit in your table-mounted router to make the cuts in the bottoms of the legs that form the feet. Raise the bit so it is slightly higher than the thickness of the legs. Position the fence so the bit makes about a ³⁄₁₆" deep cut. The majority of the bit will be behind the fence's front surface. Clamp a stop block to the fence approximately 4¾" to the left of the bit (measuring from the bit's center).

To make the cut, hold the leg flat on the table with its bottom end toward the fence. Hold the left-hand corner against the fence to the left of the bit as shown in Photo 3. Ease into the cut and push the piece until it touches the stop. Turn the piece over and repeat the process cutting the foot on the other side.

Swap the 1" bit for a ⁵⁄₁₆" straight bit. Reposition the fence so it is ⁵⁄₁₆" away from the bit. Rout two ⁵⁄₁₆" wide stopped grooves in the inside face of each of the legs to hold the front and back panels. Cut these grooves on the router table using a stop block to position the end of the cut as shown in Photos 4 and 5. The grooves should be ¼" deep, and make them in two light passes to avoid stressing the bit.

Rout two corresponding grooves in the underside of the base. Because the base is wider, you'll need to reposition the fence before making these cuts. Here, the grooves are blind at both ends, so use two stop blocks to control their start and stop points.

Mill a single piece of stock that is long enough for the two panels and somewhat wider than specified. Lay out the shape of each panel as well as the diamond pattern as shown in the Panel Detail.

THREE Because you are cutting into end grain, making the foot cut can be a little tricky. The initial part of the cut is against the grain, and the bit will have a tendency to grab. To prevent this, start sliding the piece along the fence to the left as you pivot it into the cut.

FOUR For the first cut on each leg, position the stop block 3" to the left of the bit. Make sure that the inside face of the leg is flat on the table, its side is against the fence, and the feet are pointing to the right. Make the cut by pushing the piece along the fence until it reaches the stop. Carefully lift the piece away from the bit.

FIVE With the second cut on each leg, you'll need to start at the blind end of the groove. Clamp a stop block 3" to the right of the bit. Hold the piece with its inside face down, its side against the fence, the feet pointing to the left, and the trailing edge against the stop block. This time, however, instead of having the piece flat on the table, you'll have to hold it above the bit. Start the router and pivot the piece down onto the spinning bit. Then push it to the left to cut the groove.

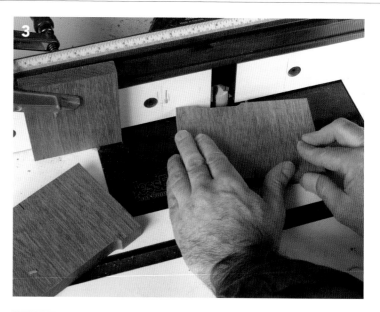

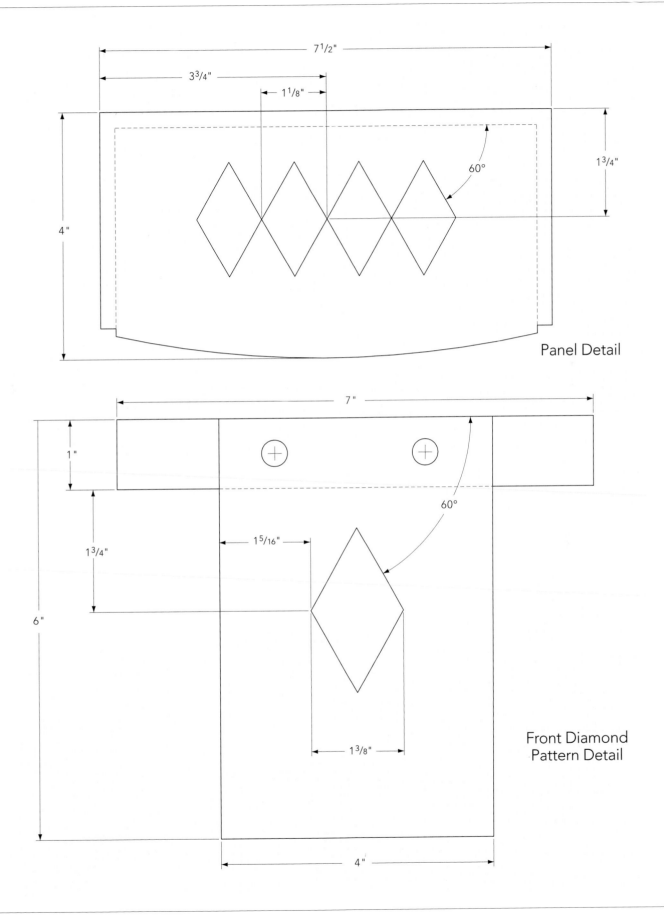

Panel Detail

Front Diamond
Pattern Detail

6

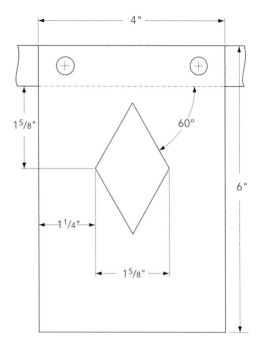

Leg Diamond
Pattern Detail

SIX The fence attached to the pattern not only serves to help locate the pattern on the panel, but also as a means of holding the pattern in place as you rout.

SEVEN The two spacers are what keep the block in place when the lamp is assembled. The grooves fit around the seam that runs down the center of the block. Once the spacers are glued in place and the top is attached, the block will be locked in place.

Make the pattern for the front diamonds from a piece of ½" MDF as shown in the Front Diamond Pattern Detail. Chuck a ⅛" straight bit in a hand-held router (I used a laminate trimmer) along with a ⅜" guide bushing. Center the pattern on each of the diamonds in turn and rout them to a depth of ⅛" as shown in Photo 6.

Make patterns for the sides and legs as shown in the Side Diamond Pattern Detail and the Leg Diamond Pattern Detail respectively. Rout the diamonds in those pieces as you did with the panels.

Cut the panels to length. Rabbet their ends and top edge on the table saw to fit in the grooves in the legs and base.

Cut the curves on the lower edge of the panels on the band saw. Sand away the saw marks.

Round the lower edges of the tongues on the ends of the panels somewhat so the width of the tongues is about ⅟₁₆" less than the length of the grooves on the legs. Do this with a chisel and/or a file.

Rabbet the lower inside edge of each panel for the bottom. The rabbets should be ⅛" wide and ⅜" deep. The easiest way to accomplish this is to use a rabbeting bit with a guide bearing big enough to limit the bit's cut to ⅛" wide. If you have such, cut the rabbets with the bit chucked in your table-mounted router and it adjusted to make a ⅜" deep cut. Hold the panels flat on the table with their outside faces up and run them against the bearing to make the cuts. If you don't have such a rabbeting bit, you can make the cut with either a fairly large straight bit (>½") or a standard, ⅜" rabbeting bit, using your table-mounted router

Cut the riser to the size given in the Materials List.

Chuck a chamfer bit in your table-mounted router and chamfer all four edges of the undersides of the top and base. Swap the bit for a ⅛" roundover bit and round over all four long grain edges on the sides and legs. Also round over all but the lower edges of the riser.

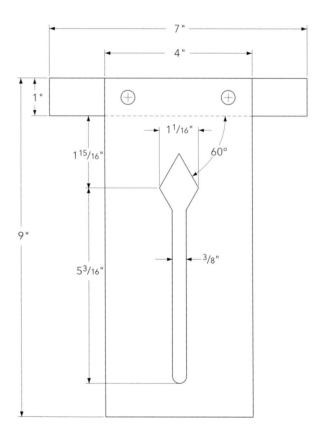

Side Diamond
Pattern Detail

7

Drill and countersink holes in the top and base so you can screw them to the sides. Also drill and counterbore the base so you can screw it to the legs. Use a ⅜" bit for the counterbores so you can plug the holes with ⅜" plugs

Cut a ⁵⁄₁₆"-wide × ³⁄₁₆"-deep groove in the inside surface of the right-hand side. Space the groove about ¾" in from the back edge. Hold the side in place on the base and mark the groove's location.

Temporarily screw the base to the sides. Drill pilot holes first to avoid splitting the wood. Place the glass block between the sides. Cut the spacers to the size given in the Materials List. Cut ³⁄₁₆" wide grooves down the centers of the spacers to accommodate the seam in the block. Fit the spacers into the spaces between the block and sides as shown in Photo 7. You'll probably need to trim them a bit to get them to fit. Once they are a snug fit, glue them to the sides.

Unscrew the sides from the base. Screw the puck holder to the underside of the base with 1" wood screws, taking care to align the 3" diameter holes with one another. Drill a ⅜"-diameter hole through both pieces centered on the mark you made at the base of the groove in the side. The groove and the hole create a path for the power cord that provides electricity to the main light. Also drill a ⅜" hole at the back of the 3" hole to provide a path for the puck's wire.

Drill a ¹³⁄₃₂" hole through the center of the top, and through center of the riser. Counterbore the underside of the top with a ¾" forstner bit. Screw the riser to the top with 1¼" woods crews.

Drill a ¾" hole through the back panel. Locate the hole as indicated in the Panel Detail. Counterbore the hole from the backside with a 1¼" bit. This is for the switch that will operate the puck light.

Cut the bottom to the size given in the Materials List. Drill a ³⁄₁₆" hole and a ¼" hole somewhere near the center for the two power cords. Check to make sure the bottom will bend to fit in the rabbets

ASSEMBLY & INSTALLATION

1. Screw the base assembly to the sides with 2" screws.
2. Feed the lamp cord through the ¼" hole in the bottom and then up through the hole that leads to the groove in the side. Pull the cord through this hole and up along the groove until you have about 9" of cord extending beyond the top of the side.
3. Thread a hex nut onto the nipple. Push the nipple up through the hole in the top/riser. Slide a bottom clamp on the exposed end of the nipple and lock it in place with a second hex nut. Thread the lamp socket onto the nipple.
4. Feed the wire up through the nipple. Split the two leads and connect it to the socket. If you are unsure about any of the electric work, consult with a licensed professional.
5. Clip the wire that is attached to the puck leaving a length about 9" long. Feed the cut end of the wire down through the hole in the base.
6. Clip the connector off the end of the wire that is attached to the transformer. Feed this end up through the ³⁄₁₆" hole in the bottom. Tie a knot in the wire to keep it from pulling back through the hole. Leave about 9" of wire to make the connections.
7. Separate the conductors on each of the two puck wires so you have four individual leads. Strip ½" of insulation off each of the leads.
8. Take a close look at the insulation on each of the leads. Two will have lettering on them, and the other two will have a series of lines. Twist the two leads with the lettering together. Solder them and cap the connection with a wire nut. Make sure there is no bare metal exposed.
9. Push the switch through the hole in the back panel and lock it in place with the included nut. Solder the remaining two leads (those with the lines on the insulation) to the switch terminals.
10. Fold any excess wire into the space at the bottom of the lamp. Screw the bottom into the rabbets in the panels with #6 x 1" wood screws.

cut into the bottom edges of the panels. If it won't, cut a series of shallow (¹⁄₁₆") kerfs across one face. Space the kerfs about ¾" apart. These should make the piece more flexible.

Seal the parts with the diamond cuts with a coat of spray shellac. Allow the shellac to dry thoroughly, then paint the triangles with acrylic artists paint. Allow the paint to dry overnight. Sand the surfaces to clean up any excess paint and shellac.

Put the panels in place and screw the base to the legs with 2" wood screws. Plug the holes and sand the plugs flush. Leave the rest of the lamp apart for now. It will be easier to finish with the pieces separate.

Finish the lamp with your favorite finish. The lamp in the photos was finished with several coats of spray shellac.

ONE DESIGN: THREE SIZES. **SMALL: JATOBA AND WENGE. MEDIUM: WALNUT. LARGE: QUARTERSAWN SYCAMORE, WALNUT.**

4 **TRAPEZOID** LAMPS

AT SEVERAL POINTS IN THIS BOOK you'll probably read that truncated pyramids and cones are among my favorite shapes. I find them both aesthetically pleasing as well as practical. From the aesthetic standpoint they are symmetrical, yet possess a definite up and down orientation. Unlike many other common geometric shapes, they seem to possess a definite beginning and end. Compare this to a rectangular block (or prism, as it is called in math class) which could easily go on and on.

I had a professor in college who talked about dealing with this perception by taking materials "out of stock." That is altering them so they lose their "extruded" look and have a pleasing, as well as logical termination. Both cones and pyramids accomplish this by being tapered. The shapes are simple, yet elegant, and make visual sense in that as your eye traces the form, the lines converge to a seemingly natural end.

From the practical point of view, tapered shapes lend themselves well to lamp design as the heavier end can be placed at the bottom where it provides stability while the smaller end provides support for the electrical components without getting in the way of the light and casting a shadow on the surface below.

This trio of lamps grew from a sketch of a floor lamp. That lamp had a pyramid for a base that supported a round column which, in turn, supported the electrical parts. I made a quick cardboard model of the base and decided it would make a great lamp on its own. After living with the model for several weeks, I decided the basic design would work for three sizes of lamps: a large lamp for use in great rooms, a medium-sized lamp for somewhat smaller spaces, and a small lamp for use in a bedroom, or other more intimate space.

The construction process for all three sizes is the same, though the sizes of the various parts are different from model to model for obvious reasons. The angles involved also vary somewhat from size to size.

Speaking of angles, the challenge in these lamps is cutting the compound angles that form the corner joints. For these, you'll need to make up a pair of carrier jigs that hold the side pieces at the correct orientation to the blade, and tilt the blade to the proper bevel angle. This is a bit fussy, but with patience and a few test pieces, I'm sure you'll get it right.

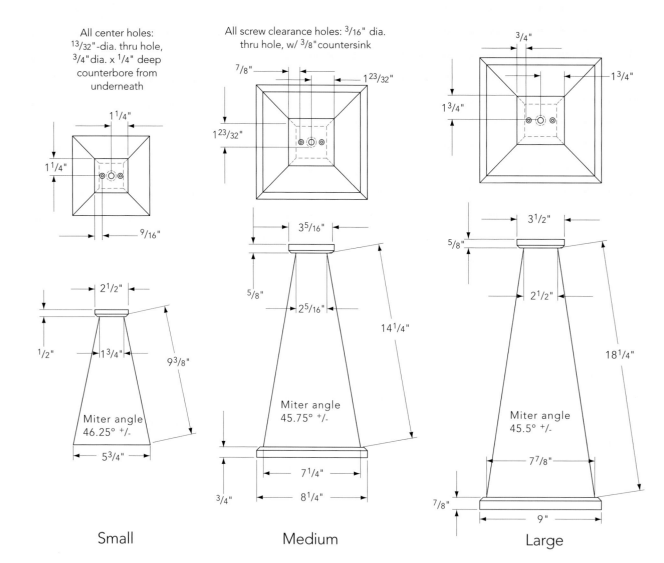

All center holes:
$^{13}/_{32}$"-dia. thru hole,
$^{3}/_{4}$"dia. x $^{1}/_{4}$" deep
counterbore from
underneath

All screw clearance holes: $^{3}/_{16}$" dia.
thru hole, w/ $^{3}/_{8}$"countersink

Small

Medium

Large

				THICKNESS		WIDTH		LENGTH	
REFERENCE	QUANTITY	PART	STOCK		(mm)		(mm)		(mm)
INCHES (MILLIMETERS)									
Small Lamp									
A	4	sides	jatoba	$^{3}/_{4}$	(19)	$5^{3}/_{4}$	(146)	$9^{3}/_{8}$	(239)
B	1	top	wenge	$^{1}/_{2}$	(13)	$2^{1}/_{2}$	(64)	$2^{1}/_{2}$	(64)
Medium Lamp									
A	4	sides	walnut	$^{3}/_{4}$	(19)	$7^{1}/_{4}$	(184)	$14^{1}/_{4}$	(362)
B	1	top	walnut	$^{5}/_{8}$	(13)	$3^{5}/_{16}$	(84)	$3^{5}/_{16}$	(84)
C	4	base moulding	walnut	$^{3}/_{4}$	(19)	3	(76)	$8^{1}/_{4}$	(209)
Big Lamp									
A	4	sides	sycamore	$^{3}/_{4}$	(19)	$7^{7}/_{8}$	(200)	$18^{1}/_{4}$	(463)
B	1	top	walnut	$^{5}/_{8}$	(13)	$3^{1}/_{2}$	(89)	$3^{1}/_{2}$	(89)
C	4	base moulding	walnut	$^{7}/_{8}$	(22)	3	(76)	9	(229)

HARDWARE (each lamp)

#8 x $1^{5}/_{8}$" Wood screws (2)

#8 x 2" Wood screws (8)
(Larger two lamps only)

$1^{1}/_{2}$" x $^{1}/_{8}$ IP Nipple

$^{1}/_{8}$ IP Hex nuts (2)

Bottom Clamp

Lamp Socket w/ Switch

Lamp Cord

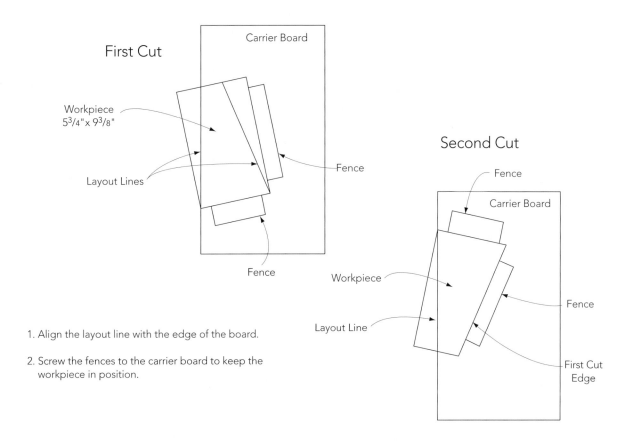

First Cut

Carrier Board

Workpiece
5³/4" x 9³/8"

Layout Lines

Fence

Fence

Second Cut

Fence

Carrier Board

Workpiece

Fence

Layout Line

First Cut
Edge

1. Align the layout line with the edge of the board.

2. Screw the fences to the carrier board to keep the workpiece in position.

Fabrication

Cut the side pieces to the size given in the Materials List. The exact thickness isn't critical, but the width and length are.

Lay out a vertical centerline on the face of one of the pieces. Choose one end to be the top and lay out the narrower width of the piece along that edge. Be sure to center your layout on the centerline. Draw the two angles on the face of the workpiece. Extend these lines down the top end of the piece using a square to keep your lines perpendicular to the face.

Cut two pieces of sheet stock to serve as bases for the two carrier jigs you'll need to make the tapered cuts. I usually use ½" MDF, but any flat sheet stock will work. Make the pieces about 10" wide and about 5-6" longer than the length of the sides.

Place the workpiece on the carrier board so the left-hand layout line aligns with the left edge of the carrier board as shown above. Screw two fences to the jig to hold the piece in this alignment. Note: if you have a right-tilting table saw, make up the

Tools Cutting compound miters requires setting the tilt on your table saw to very precise angles. One of the best tools I've found for this is called a Bevel Boss. When used in conjunction with an accurate tee bevel, you can obtain settings down to around a quarter of a degree.

jig so the right-hand layout line aligns with the right side of the jig.

Tilt the blade on your table saw to the angle indicated in the illustrations as Miter Angle for the size lamp you are making. Position the fence so the saw cuts right along your layout line as shown in Photo 1.

Make up a second carrier jig. This time, one of the fences will be ahead of the workpiece. Again, if you have a right-tilting table saw, make a mirror image of the jig in the illustration.

Reset the saw fence to cut along the second layout line as shown in Photo 2.

Hold the four sides together to check the fit of the miters. If necessary tweak the blade tilt on your saw and recut both sides of each piece. If things look pretty close, you can always make minor adjustments with a sharp hand plane.

Cut four pieces of ¼" plywood into triangles that are about ¾" narrower than the sides. Rip the cutoffs from the tapering process into strips about 1¼" wide. Screw these

ONE Hold the workpiece firmly against the fences of your carrier jig as you push it through the cut. To position the fence, cut wide of your line at first, then bump the fence over until the cut is right on the line.

TWO Make the second cut on each of the sides with the blade at the same angle.

THREE Taking the time to make up clamping blocks makes gluing up compound miters a lot easier. The beveled pieces are cut from the cutoffs that came from making the miter cuts to begin with. Using these blocks allows you to put pressure directly across the joints.

TIP Visible Layout Lines

When making layouts on dark colored wood, add a layer of masking tape to the surface and make your lines on the tape.

FOUR Because the clamp blocks are not attached to the assembly, it is the opposing pressure from all the clamps that holds things together. As you tighten things, work your way around the piece, gradually increasing the pressure to bring pieces together.

FIVE Once the sides are glued, trim their bottom edges so the assembly will sit flat. This is a compound cut made with both the blade and the miter gauge tilted away from square. Set a stop block to help keep everything even.

along the edges of the plywood triangles as shown in Photo 3.

Dry clamp the sides together, checking for a good fit. The clamping blocks are not attached to the sides, so you'll need to slowly tighten the clamps to keep everything centered. If you have someone available, now is a good time to ask for help. Start at the bottom and snug all four clamps up as you work your way around. Then repeat the process at the top as shown in Photo 4. Finally add a third set of clamps around the middle.

Once you are satisfied with the way things fit, glue the four sides together. Again, if you can get some help, it is worth it. Be aware that the glue will act as a lubricant and allow things to slip around until all the clamps are tight.

While the glue is drying, cut the material for the top and base moulding to size. (Note: I didn't put base moulding on the small lamp. It didn't seem to need it.) For the larger two lamps, I cut a single length of wood long enough for all four pieces and chamfered it before cutting the miters on the individual pieces.

Chuck a chamfer bit in your table-mounted router and chamfer the underside

of the top piece and one edge of the base moulding.

Drill a $^{13}/_{32}$" hole through the center of the top. On the underside of the piece, counterbore this hole ¼" deep with a ¾" Forstner bit. Also drill and countersink two $^3/_{16}$" holes through the top so you can screw it to the base. The placement of these holes is shown in the illustrations.

Once the glue has dried, remove the clamps from the side glue-up and scrape away any squeeze-out. The next step is to cut the bottom and top of the assembly so all four pieces are flush and true with each other. This requires angling your miter gauge and tilting the blade on your table saw. Set your miter gauge first. Rather than relying on measurements, I simply placed the assembly with one side down on the saw and used it like a big tee bevel. Hold it against the blade and adjust the miter gauge to match the side taper angle. Then tilt the blade so it matches the side tilt angle. Cut the bottom edges of all four sides as shown in Photo 5 on the preceding page.

Switch the miter gauge to the other side of the blade and trim the top end as shown in Photo 6. If you're making the small lamp, you may need to drill a ½" hole down through the center where the sides come together to allow clearance for the cord.

Cut the pieces of the base moulding to length by mitering their ends at 45°. The exact length isn't critical, you just want the base to protrude about ½" beyond the side assembly on all four sides.

Cut biscuit slots in both mitered ends of all four side pieces as shown in Photo 7. Offset the cuts to the inside of the pieces so you can use a #20 biscuit without the cut coming through the outside face of the moulding. Glue up the four pieces to form a square frame.

Drill and countersink two $^3/_{16}$" holes per side through the pieces of the base frame. Sand everything, then center the base on the side assembly and screw them together with 2" Screws. Pick the best looking side to be the front. Drill a $^5/_{16}$" hole through the opposite side for the cord. Center the hole and locate it about 1" up from the base/side junction.

Finish all the parts. I used Minwax Antique Oil finish, a wiping varnish.

SIX Switch the miter gauge to the opposite side of the blade to trim the top end. The miter gauge angle and the blade tilt remain the same as for the bottom cuts. The top end is narrow enough, you can probably trim it in a single pass with the blade on your saw raised.

SEVEN Reinforce the miter joints in the base with biscuits. Make the layout mark about ¼" off center so you don't have to worry about the cutter coming through the face of the moulding.

ASSEMBLY & INSTALLATION

1. Thread a nut on one end of the pipe nipple and slide the nipple up through the center hole in the top. Slip a bottom clamp on the nipple and lock it in place with a second nut.
2. Poke the end of the cord through the hole in the back of the lamp and feed it up through the hole at the top of the sides. Thread the cord through the nipple.
3. Screw the top to the sides. Then attach the cord to the socket as described in the Electrical section on page 8.
4. As a final touch, glue a square of felt to the underside of the base. Add a harp, shade, and bulb then put your lamp into service. Note: Always take your lamp with you when you go shopping for shades. It will enjoy the outing and it is much easier to decide when you can actually try the shade on for size.

SUBTLE TAPERS AND GENTLE CURVES LEND THIS DESK LAMP AN AIR OF MODERN SOPHISTICATION AND ELEGANCE.
WHITE OAK

5 **SLEEK TASK** LAMP

THE WARMTH OF HARDWOOD combines with clean lines and up-to-date technology to make this a contemporary task light that is elegant, yet completely practical. As I was working on this design, I was thinking about a number of the contemporary desk lamps I've seen that make use of spindly metal tubes, springs and articulated joints. These types of materials don't really lend themselves to woodworking. However, it was the simple, crisp look that I was after.

As with most designs, I went through a lot of sketches before arriving at the lamp presented here. My goals were to use a minimum number of parts; to keep those parts very simple yet elegant forms; and to use off-the-shelf electrical components to keep fabrication and assembly fairly straightforward. I'm pretty satisfied with the end results. About the only thing that I'm still pondering is the spine that covers the wiring.

I believe in making things that can be disassembled for repair. So the wire leading from the base up to the lamp has to remain accessible. My solution of screwing the spine in place to cover the wiring groove works. The screws are small, unobtrusive, and provide good access. But as I write this, I'm wondering if there isn't a more elegant way to go about this ... some kind of tapered sliding dovetail, perhaps. Oh well, it is good to have something to try on the next version.

As for function, the lamp makes use of a 3" LED puck light. I used these on several of the lamps in this book. They throw a nice, bright light, don't use a lot of electricity, don't generate a lot of heat, and last a long time (up to twenty years according to the manufacturer). About the only drawback is they require a transformer to be plugged into the wall outlet. The presence of the transformer isn't that big a deal. The real problem is that these little buggers act as power vampires, using a small amount of current whenever they are plugged in, whether the lamp they are attached to is on or not. The amount of electricity consumed is trivial, but it adds up. This problem doesn't stop me from using LED lights, but it does make me ponder a solution.

With regard to construction, you'll be cutting and gluing a miter joint, tapering pieces, and drilling a handful of holes. The electrical system is pretty simply, requiring only that you install a switch in the wire that feeds the LED assembly.

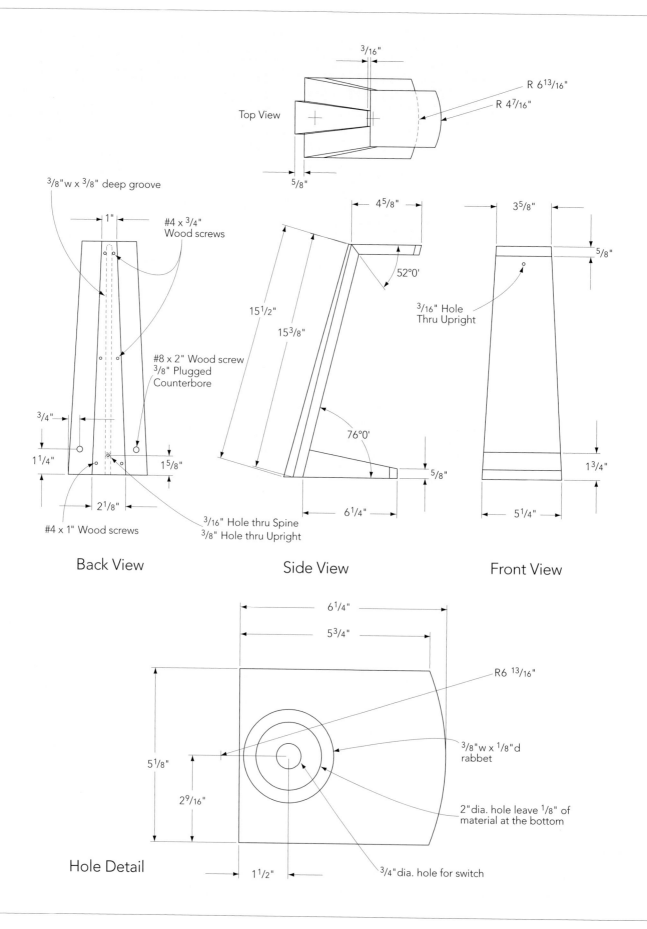

Top View

3/16"

R 6¹³/₁₆"

R 4⁷/₁₆"

5/8"

3/8"w x 3/8" deep groove

1"

#4 x 3/4"
Wood screws

4⁵/₈"

52°0'

3⁵/₈"

5/8"

3/16" Hole
Thru Upright

15¹/₂"

15³/₈"

#8 x 2" Wood screw
3/8" Plugged
Counterbore

76°0'

3/4"

1¹/₄"

1⁵/₈"

5/8"

1³/₄"

2¹/₈"

6¹/₄"

5¹/₄"

#4 x 1" Wood screws

3/16" Hole thru Spine
3/8" Hole thru Upright

Back View

Side View

Front View

6¹/₄"

5³/₄"

R6 ¹³/₁₆"

5¹/₈"

2⁹/₁₆"

3/8"w x 1/8"d
rabbet

2"dia. hole leave 1/8" of
material at the bottom

Hole Detail

1¹/₂"

3/4"dia. hole for switch

INCHES (MILLIMETERS)

REFERENCE	QUANTITY	PART	STOCK	THICKNESS	(mm)	WIDTH	(mm)	LENGTH	(mm)
A	1	upright	white oak	5/8	(16)	5 1/4	(133)	15 3/8	(391)
B	1	top	white oak	5/8	(16)	3 3/4	(95)	4 5/8	(118)
C	1	base	white oak	1 3/4	(45)	5 1/4	(133)	6 1/4	(158)
D	1	cover plate	white oak	1/8	(3)	2 3/4	(70)	dia.	
E	1	spine	white oak	5/8	(16)	2 1/8	(54)	15 1/2	(394)
F	2	plugs	white oak			3/8	(10)	dia.	

HARDWARE

8 x 2" Wood Screws (2)

4 x 1" Wood Screws (2)

#4 x 3/4" Wood Screws (4)

LED Puck Light Kit
(Hampton Bay # 957 245)

SPST Rocker Switch
(Radio Shack #275-0693)

Wire Nut

Felt Feet (4)

Fabrication

Cut a piece of stock to the thickness and width of the upright listed in the Materials List, but make it long enough so you can get both the upright and top piece out of it. After surfacing the piece, cut both the upright and top to length. Also cut a piece of stock for the base to the size listed.

Tilt the blade on your table saw to 52° and miter the mating ends of the upright and top as shown in Photo 1.

Reset the angle of the blade to 76° and cross cut the opposite end of the upright and one end of the base at this new angle.

Chuck a 3/8" straight bit in your table-mounted router and cut a 5/16"-deep groove in the outside face of the upright. The groove should be centered from side to side, and stop 3/8" from the upper end of the piece. The groove can run out through the lower end.

Set the fence on your biscuit joiner to match the miter angle and cut matching biscuit slots in mitered faces of both the top and the upright as shown in Photo 2. Center the slots from side to side.

ONE Make the angled cuts by pushing the pieces past the blade with the miter gauge. If you keep the pieces in order, you can make the grain appear to wrap around the corner.

TWO Clamp the pieces down to your bench when you cut the biscuit slots. Use a piece of 1/4" plywood as a clamping pad as well as the reference surface for the biscuit joiner's fence. This will move the position of the slot up the mitered face to where the material is thicker.

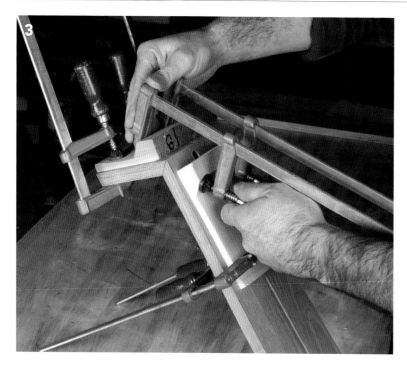

THREE Using specially-made, angled clamping blocks allows you to apply clamping pressure perpendicular to miter joint.

FOUR Cleaning up the tapered face of the base is a great excuse to break out a hand plane. With a sharp iron, it shouldn't take more than a few minutes to clean up the saw marks.

Lay out a center line on the inside face of the upright. Draw angled lines to indicate how the piece tapers. It should go from full width at the bottom to 3¾" at the top. Make the taper equal on both sides. Cut along your layout lines on the band saw then smooth away the saw marks with a plane.

Cut the top down in width so it is slightly wider than top of the upright. Be sure to remove the waste equally from both sides so the biscuit slot remains centered. Mark the curve on the outside end of the top. Cut it to shape on the band saw. Sand the curve to remove the saw marks and give the top a slight bevel.

Make up some angled clamping blocks as shown in Photo 3. Cut these on the band saw from pieces of scrap. The angles should more or less match the miter angles, but close is probably good enough. Clamp the blocks to the top and to the upright. Dry fit the pieces to make sure everything fits right and the blocks are in the correct position. When everything looks good, glue the pieces together — don't forget to add the biscuit.

Lay out the base's taper on its side. It should taper from 1¾" thick at the top of the angled cut to approximately ⅝" at the opposite end as shown in the Side View. Make the cut on the band saw, then clean up the sawn surface with a hand plane as shown in Photo 4.

Lay out the curve along the thinner edge of the base. Cut along the line with the band saw as shown in Photo 5. Sand the curve to refine its shape and remove the saw marks.

Hold the base in place against the upright. Trace the upright's taper onto the base, then use a hand plane to bevel the sides of the base so they match the taper. Plane the sides of the top to match the taper as well.

Drill a 2" diameter hole, angled 76°, in the underside of the base, so that it is perpendicular to the top surface of the base as indicated in the Hole Detail. The hole is angled so the switch will sit flush on the top of the base. Make the hole deep enough so that only about ⅛" of material remains before the hole would break through the top surface.

This creates a compartment for the wiring. Drill a ¾" hole for the switch through the top surface, centering this hole inside the 2" hole.

Chuck a rabbeting bit in your table-mounted router and cut a ⅜"-wide × ⅛"-deep rabbet around the 2" hole you just drilled as shown in Photo 6. This creates a recess for the cover plate that will protect the wiring.

Drill ³⁄₁₆" holes through the upright for the screws that will fasten it to the base. Drill ⅜"-diameter × ¼"-deep counterbores for wooden plugs to cover the screw heads. Hold the upright in position against the base. Drill ⅛" pilot holes and screw the two pieces together with #8 × 1½" wood screws. Plug the holes and sand the plugs flush.

Cut the cover plate so it fits into the rabbet in the bottom of the base. Drill and countersink for two #6 × ⅝" wood screws to hold the cover plate in place. You can make the cover plate from either solid wood cut to ⅛" thickness or from a piece of ⅛" plywood.

Cut the spine to the size given in the Materials List. Cut the ends off at 76° making the piece a parallelogram.

Taper the spine in width from 2⅛" at the bottom to 1" at the top. Cut the waste off both sides to keep the piece symmetrical. Also taper the piece in thickness from ⅝" at the bottom to ³⁄₁₆" at the top. Make these cuts on the band saw and clean up the sawn edges with a hand plane.

Drill and countersink six holes along the edges of the spines for the screws that will hold it in place as shown in the Back View. Also drill two ³⁄₁₆" holes for the wires to pass through; one in the spine about 1¼" up from the bottom and the other in the upright just below the miter joint between it and the top. Both holes should be centered from side to side. Also drill a ⅜" hole through the upright into the big hole you drilled in the base. This hole is also spaced about 1¼" up from the bottom, and centered within the groove.

Finish the lamp with your favorite wood finish. The lamp in the photos is finished with several coats of Waterlox Transparent, a wiping varnish.

FIVE Cut a curve along the front edge of the base to make the base's shape echo that of the top.

SIX To cut the rabbet around the hole, just drop the base down over the bit and let the bearing ride against the hole's wall. Rotate the base in a counterclockwise direction as you make the cut.

ASSEMBLY & INSTALLATION

1. Cut the connector off of the wire that comes from the puck. Push the cut end of the wire through the hole at the top of the upright.

2. Screw the puck to the underside of the top. Push the cut end of the wire through the hole at the bottom of the upright and into the big hole in the base. Work out the slack so the wire lies neatly in the groove. Cut off the excess, leaving an end about 6" long to make the connections.

3. Cut the connector off the wire attached to the transformer. Push the cut end through the hole in the bottom of the spine and then through the hole that leads into the big hole in the bottom of the base. Note: At this point the spine hasn't been attached to the upright. Make sure the transformer is on the outer side of the spine. Don't ask why I bother to point this out, but if you get things mixed up, you'll have to redo all the connections.

4. Tie a loose overhand knot in the wire so it can't pull back through the hole. Leave about 6" of wire free to make the connections. The knot is there to protect the connections should someone pull on the wire.

5. Split the wires apart so you have four separate leads. Strip about ½" of insulation off each end. Look carefully at the individual wires. Two will have lettering on them, and two will have a series of dashes. It is important to connect like to like, or the LEDs won't work. Twist the two leads with lettering on them together. Solder the junction and cap it with a wire nut. Make sure the cap completely covers any exposed metal.

6. Push the switch through the hole in the base and fasten it in place with the nut that came with it. Fasten the other two leads to the terminals on the switch. Twist the ends back on themselves, then solder the connections.

7. Tuck all the wire into the big hole and screw the cover plate in place. Also screw the spine to the upright. Apply four felt feet to the underside of the lamp as a finishing touch.

WHEN YOU WANT TO GET AWAY FROM THE EARTH TONES COMMON TO SO MANY WOODWORKING PROJECTS, CONSIDER USING DYES TO CREATE A BRIGHTER LOOK. **MAPLE, TRANS TINT DYES**

6 KRAZY QUILT LAMP

HAVING GROWN UP WITH GRANDPARENTS who were weavers and a mother who quilts, I guess I shouldn't be surprised that I have an appreciation for geometric patterns. I've dabbled with including such in my woodworking for years, mainly through inlaying contrasting species of wood. I have also played a little with color, mixing different colors of wood as well as dying wood with aniline dyes. The first color dyes I had were powders meant for dying textiles. These worked well, but weren't especially easy to work with, requiring careful mixing to get consistent results.

A year or three ago I stumbled upon Trans Tint dyes. These come in a concentrated liquid form. They are quite easy to mix with either water or alcohol. While somewhat expensive, they have made the process of dying wood to create vivid colors much more straightforward.

With this lamp, I was trying to pick up on the idea of panels assembled from geometric shapes similar to the way quilts and stained glass windows are designed. I also drew inspiration from a somewhat strange source: Taco Bell. Many of these restaurants in my area have recently undergone facelifts. Part of their new look includes colored stucco panels that are cut across with seemingly random lines that create irregular triangles.

There are all sorts of possibilities beyond what I show here. On my next version of this lamp I definitely want to design each of the four panels so the lines and patterning flow from one surface to the next.

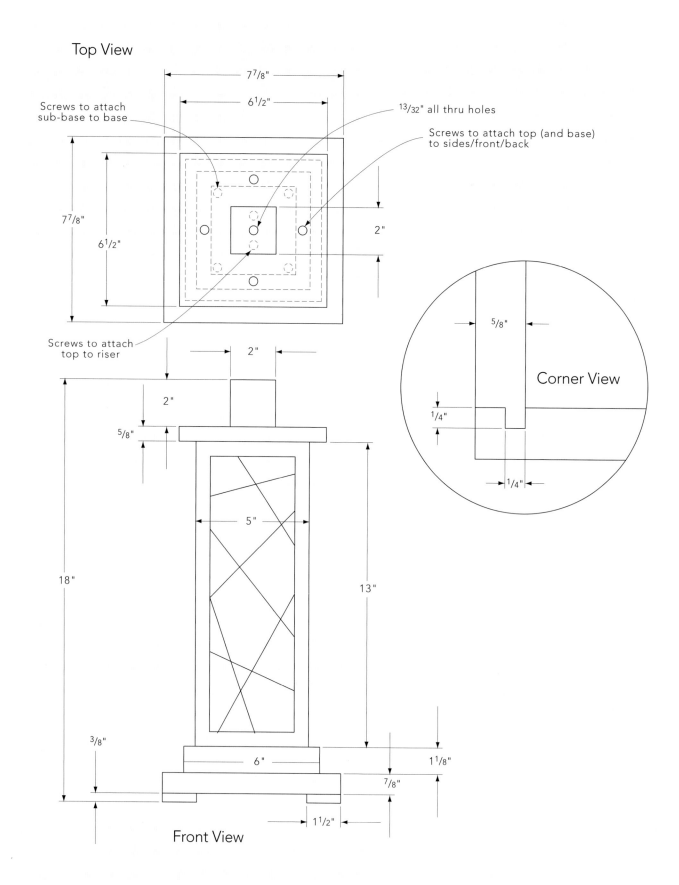

Top View

Screws to attach
sub-base to base

$^{13}/_{32}$" all thru holes

Screws to attach top (and base)
to sides/front/back

7$^7/_8$"

6$^1/_2$"

7$^7/_8$"

6$^1/_2$"

2"

Screws to attach
top to riser

2"

2"

$^5/_8$"

5 "

18 "

13 "

Corner View

$^5/_8$"

$^1/_4$"

$^1/_4$"

$^3/_8$"

6 "

1$^1/_8$"

$^7/_8$"

1$^1/_2$"

Front View

INCHES (MILLIMETERS)

REFERENCE	QUANTITY	PART	STOCK	THICKNESS	(mm)	WIDTH	(mm)	LENGTH	(mm)
A	2	sides	maple	5/8	(16)	4 1/4	(108)	13	(330)
B	2	front/back	maple	5/8	(16)	5	(127)	13	(330)
C	1	riser	maple	2	(51)	2	(51)	2	(51)
D	1	top	maple	5/8	(16)	6 1/2	(165)	6 1/2	(165)
E	1	base	maple	1 1/8	(29)	6	(152)	6	(152)
F	1	sub-base	maple	7/8	(22)	7 7/8	(200)	7 7/8	(200)
G	4	feet	maple	3/8	(10)	1 1/2	(38)	1 1/2	(38)

HARDWARE

8 x 1 5/8" Wood Screws (6)
#8 x 2" Wood Screws (4)
#8 x 2 1/2" Wood Screws (4)
1/8 IP x 3 1/2" Nipple
1/8 IP Hex Nuts (2)
Bottom Clamp
Lamp Socket w/ Switch
Lamp Cord
Felt

Fabrication

Cut the pieces for the front, back, and sides to the dimensions listed in the Materials List.

The sides are joined to the front and back with tongue-and-groove joints. The joints aren't necessary for strength, they just help keep things in alignment when you are gluing up. Set up a 1/4"-wide dado head on your table saw and adjust its height to 1/4". Adjust the fence so the distance from it to the outside of the dado is just a hair more than the thickness of the sides. Cut two grooves in one face of both the front and back as shown in Photo 1.

Increase the width of the dado to 1/2" (+/- the exact size isn't critical) and lower it a hair. (See Shop Tip, below.) Reposition the fence so the distance between it and the inside of the blade is slightly more than 1/4". Cut the tongues on the sides with the pieces held on edge against the fence as shown in Photo 2.

ONE Choose the best face on both the front and back pieces. Keep this face up as you cut the dadoes in each of the pieces.

TWO To cut the mating tongue, start by cutting a tongue that is too thick. Bump the fence over and recut, repeating the process until the tongue fits snugly in the groove.

SHOP TIP When cutting tongue-and-groove joints, make the tongue's length slightly (1/32+") less than the depth of the groove. This way the joint will still go together even if there is debris in the groove, or the groove's depth isn't consistent.

Lay out the patterns on the front, back, and sides as shown in the Pattern Details. The exact placement of the diagonal lines isn't critical, put them where you think they belong. The placement of the rectangular borders is somewhat more important, if only for the sake of consistency from face to face. I drew the lines with a Sharpie both so they would show up well in the photo and so I see how the finished piece would look before cutting. While I wouldn't want to use such a thick line for cutting joints, it worked fine for this application.

Rout the lines with a 60° vee bit chucked in a hand-held router as shown in Photo 3. Use a ½" guide bushing to guide the router along a straightedge. Rout the pattern lines on all four pieces in this manner.

Glue the four pieces together to form a square tube. After the glue dries, rout the final lines on the sides right along the glue lines.

Sand the lines to clean up after the router. I tried one of the rubber "tadpole" sanding blocks but found that its corners crumbled too quickly. Instead I cut a scrap to a thickness of ⅛" and handplaned one edge to 60° to match the router bit. Then I wrapped the paper around this pointy edge.

Spray the tube assembly with several coats of shellac to serve as a sealer. Then spray the lines with black spray paint as shown in Photo 4.

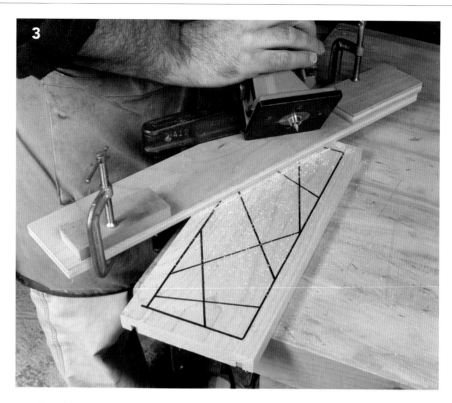

Allow the paint to dry thoroughly then plane, scrape and sand all four surfaces of the tube to clean them up as shown in Photo 5.

Cut the pieces for the top, riser, base and sub-base to the sizes given in the Materials List. Drill a ¹³⁄₃₂" hole through the center of each piece.

THREE Clamp a straightedge parallel to the line you're cutting with stops clamped at either end. If you're using a ½" guide bushing, the straightedge should be offset from the line by ¼".

Pattern Details

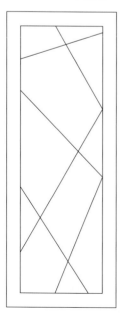
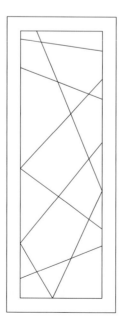
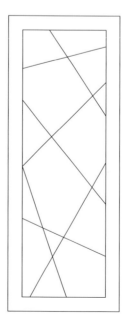
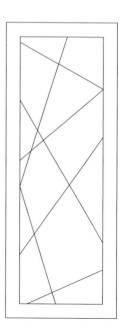

FOUR To color in the lines, it is easiest to use spray paint. I used flat black because I had it, but gloss will work as well. Don't worry about spraying the surrounding surfaces, you'll sand them clean later.

FIVE I find it somewhat magical to watch the lines appear as I clean up the painted surfaces. I used a handplane, but a random orbit sander would work just as well.

Cut the feet to the size listed and glue them to the four corners of the sub-base.

Drill two ³⁄₁₆" clearance holes through the top and countersink them from the underside. Screw the top to the riser with 1⅝" wood screws, keeping the center holes aligned. Drill pilot ³⁄₃₂" pilot holes in the riser to keep it from splitting.

Drill and countersink the appropriate holes in the top, base, and sub-base. Screw the base to the bottom end of the tube assembly with 2½" wood screws. Screw the top to its upper end with 2" wood screws. And screw the sub-base to the base with 1⅝" screws. Be sure to drill pilot holes and to keep all the pieces centered.

Plan your color scheme. Dilute the TransTint dyes with alcohol to the color intensity you are after. I keep a piece of scrap handy on which to test the colors. Be sure to sand the scrap to the same degree to which you sanded the good pieces so the dyes absorb in a similar manner. I apply the dyes to small areas such as these with cotton swabs. When you are happy with your colors, dye all four panels.

Allow the dyes to thoroughly dry, then apply a clear top coat. I sprayed on several coats of lacquer and then rubbed out the finish to a satin sheen.

Glue felt squares to the bottoms of the feet as a finishing touch.

ASSEMBLY

1. Separate the top from the tube/base assembly. Slide the nipple up through the center hole. Thread on a hex nut from the underside and a bottom clamp and a second hex nut from the top. Tighten the nuts to lock everything in place. Thread on the bottom part of a light socket.
2. Push the end of the lamp cord up through the hole in the sub-base. Pull the cord up and push the end through the nipple. Separate the two leads and tie them in a knot before connecting them to the terminals on the socket. Refer to the Electrical Section on p. 8 for specifics as to how to make the connections. If you aren't comfortable with the electric end of things, consult with a licensed professional.
3. Add a harp and a shade and your lamp will be ready to go. Take it with you when you go shopping for shades — it is much easy to judge how they look when you have the lamp right there.

THE STEPPED LAYERS AND CHEVRON-LIKE ANGLES IN THE BASE COMBINE WITH THE GENTLE CURVES OF THE GLASS BLOCK TO GIVE THIS LAMP A DISTINCTIVE ART DECO FEELING. **CHERRY**

⑦ **DECO** LAMP

THE DESIGN FOR THIS LAMP started when I stumbled upon the collection of glass blocks for sale in my local home center. I was so taken with them that I walked out of the store that evening with a pretty good assortment to play with. This lamp is the third one I made that incorporates one of the blocks I bought. Unlike the Lighthouse Lamp and Harlequin Lamp, the glass block here is meant to be the a primary light source — one you would use to light up a room. In the other two designs, the glass blocks serve as nightlights. In all three designs, the illumination comes from LED puck lamps.

I had a pretty good idea of how I wanted to use this corner block by the time I got it back to my shop — held diagonally in a vee-shaped base with the pucks lighting it up from below. Unfortunately, I quickly found a flaw in my plan. As purchased, the block was clear with a slightly wavy appearance to the glass. When I tried shining the LEDs up through it, the light beams just passed on through and made two spots on the ceiling much as a pair of flashlights might produce. Interesting, but not the effect I was after. I wanted the block to glow. In order to make this happen, I needed a frosted surface rather than a clear one.

After checking to see if I could purchase a frosted block (I couldn't, Pittsburgh Corning doesn't seem to make this style with a frosted finish.) I broke out my sandblaster to see if I could frost the thing myself. It proved remarkably easy. I just set the block in the grass outside my shop and blasted away. About 10 minutes later I was done.

Once the problem with the glass was solved, the rest of the design came together pretty quickly. The block itself suggested that the lamp have an Art Deco flair. Hence the stepped appearance of the many layers. The moulding surrounding the block serves to lock the block in place. To facilitate finishing, as well as repair (the block will break if it falls on a hard floor) the pieces are screwed in place and the screw heads are left accessible so you can take things apart if necessary. Actually, much of the rest of the lamp is screwed together as well and can be easily disassembled should you need to get at the wiring or replace the LEDs.

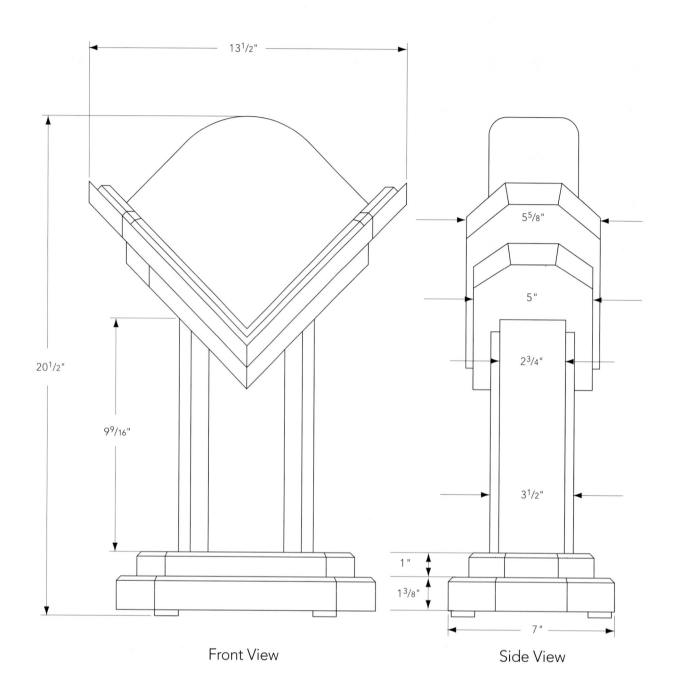

Front View

Side View

HARDWARE

Decora Encurve Finishing Unit (Corner Glass Block - Pittsburgh Corning)

#20 Biscuits (2)

#8 x 1" Wood Screws (20)

#8 x 1 1/4" Wood Screws (2)

#8 x 1 5/8" Wood Screws (4)

#8 x 2" Wood Screws (4)

#8 x 2 1/2" Wood Screws (4)

3-Light LED Puck Light Kit (Hampton Bay #980)

SPST Rocker Switch (Radio Shack #275-0693)

Wire nuts (2)

Fabrication

While you don't have to do this first, it is a great way to get started. Sand blast the glass block to give it a frosted look as shown in Photo 1. For sandblasting, I use a cheap plastic unit from Campbell Hausfield. As I recall, I found it online for about $30. If you don't have access to compressed air (or a place to blast — it is a bit messy) you can probably take your block to an autobody shop or a welding place and have them do it for you.

Cut the main and lower vee pieces to the thickness and width given in the Materials List, but leave them slightly longer than necessary. Then cut the stock for the side and end mouldings to the width and thickness listed, but leave the pieces 2" or so too long for now. Chuck a 45° chamfer bit in a table-mounted router and chamfer one corner of each side moulding piece.

Place the glass block on top of one of the end moulding pieces so that the block overlaps the wooden piece by ¾". Trace around the block as shown in Photo 2. Repeat with the second end moulding piece, using the other side of the block.

ONE Sandblast the glass until it has an even, frosted appearance. Be sure to wear a full face shield to protect yourself.

TWO Transfer the shape of the glass onto the end moulding pieces by tracing along the glass. Lay out a center line on each of the moulding pieces and align it with the center ridge cast into the block.

TIP As you get ready to sand blast, make sure you use dry sand and sift it to eliminate any larger chunks that may clog the nozzle. I keep an old window screen on hand for this purpose.

INCHES (MILLIMETERS)

REFERENCE	QUANTITY	PART	STOCK	THICKNESS	(mm)	WIDTH	(mm)	LENGTH	(mm)
A	2	main vee pieces	cherry	⅝	(16)	5⅝	(143)	9⅝	(245)
B	2	lower vee pieces	cherry	⅝	(16)	5	(127)	7⅞	(200)
C	4	side mouldings	cherry	½	(13)	½	(13)	7½	(191)
D	2	end mouldings	cherry	½	(13)	3⅞	(98)	1½	(38)
E	2	wide uprights	cherry	⅝	(16)	3½	(89)	9	(229)
F	2	narrow uprights	cherry	⅝	(16)	2¾	(70)	9½	(242)
G	1	plinth	cherry	1	(25)	5¼	(133)	9¼	(235)
H	1	base	cherry	1⅜	(35)	7	(178)	11	(279)
I	4	feet	cherry	¼	(6)	1	(25)	1	(25)

Cut along the tracing line on the band saw. Use a round file to refine the shape if necessary to make the moulding fit well against the glass. Make the two angled cuts on the outside of the moulding on the band saw as well. True up these cuts with a stationary belt or disk sander.

Chamfer the outside edges of the end mouldings to match the chamfer on the side moulding pieces. Use a block plane to make these cuts as shown in Photo 3.

The end moulding pieces are too small and fragile to risk chamfering on a router table. Instead, break out your block plane and go at it by hand. A sharp block plane makes quite short work of creating a chamfer.

Choose one end of each of the main vee pieces to be mitered. From those ends, measure in a distance equal to the thickness of the pieces and draw lines perpendicular to the sides to indicate the top of the miter cuts.

Lay out a center line along the length of each of the pieces. Position the glass block on one of the pieces, aligning its square corner with the line you just drew and centering it from side to side.

Cut one end of each piece of side moulding to match the angles on the end mouldings. Cut chamfers on these ends to match those on the end mouldings.

Set the mouldings in place, surrounding the glass block and trace around them to mark their locations as shown in Photo 4. Repeat the process

THREE Because of the fragile, end-grain orientation of the end moulding pieces, a block plane is the preferable tool for chamfering.

FOUR Use the glass block to help determine the placement of the mouldings. Trace around the pieces to mark their places on the vee pieces.

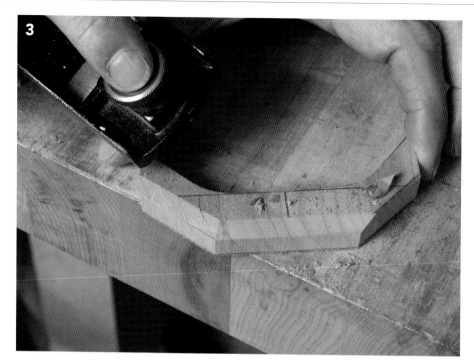

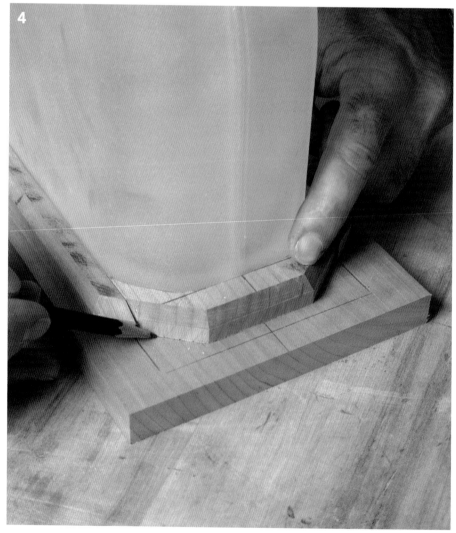

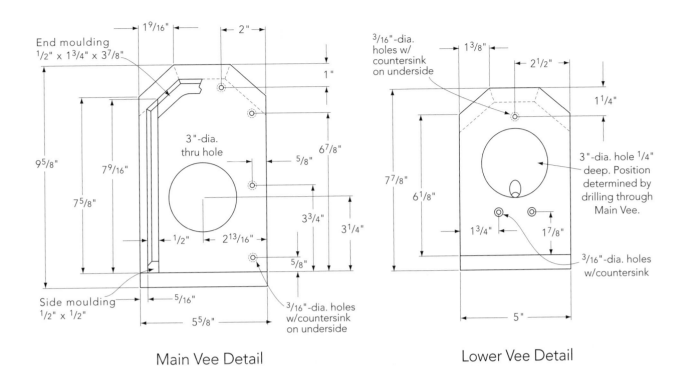

Main Vee Detail

Lower Vee Detail

to locate the mouldings on the second of the main vee pieces.

Drill and countersink holes through the main pieces as indicated in the Main Vee Detail. Screw the side mouldings in place and make sure the glass block fits in between them. If the fit is too tight, remove the mouldings and trim a little off the inside edges before reattaching them.

Make the angled cuts on the outside ends of the main vee pieces as indicated in the Main Vee Detail. I made these cuts on the band saw and then used a stationary belt sander to bevel each of them at 45°.

Tilt the blade on your table saw to 45° and cut the miters on the inside ends of the main vee pieces as shown in Photo 5.

FIVE Cutting the vee pieces with the moulding attached means the mouldings will come together in a perfect (hopefully) miter as well as the vee pieces themselves.

Now glue the two main vee pieces together as shown in Photo 6. While you have the blade on your table saw tilted, cut the lower vee pieces to length, mitering the ends at the same time. Note: the angled cuts should be in the same direction, making the pieces into parallelograms as shown in the Front View. Glue these pieces together as you did with the main vee pieces.

After the glue dries in both of the vee assemblies, cut grooves for splines across the joints. Hold the pieces in a vee-shaped cradle as shown in Photo 7 as you run them past the blade. Make four cuts in each vee. The outer cuts should be placed about ¾" in from the edges and the inner cut about another ¾" inside the first ones. Treat the assemblies gently as you handle them. The miter joints won't be very strong until you have reinforced them with splines with the grain running across the joint.

Cut the corners off the outer ends of the lower vee pieces as shown in the Lower Vee Detail. Bevel these cuts at 45° as you did with the corner cuts on the main vee pieces.

SIX When gluing miters, it helps to make up clamping blocks that allow you to put clamping pressure perpendicular to the joint. Cut these blocks on the band saw and clamp them to the workpieces.

SEVEN Make up a vee cradle to help hold the vee assemblies in the proper orientation as you cut the slots for the splines. Be sure to keep any screws well above the range of the saw blade.

Drill and countersink the screw holes in the lower vee assembly. Screw the two vee assemblies together. Drill 3" diameter holes through the main vee pieces and into the lower vee pieces as shown in Photo 8. The holes should be centered from side-to-side and located 3¼" up from the corner.

Cut the pieces for the base and plinth to the sizes indicated in the Materials List. Also cut the wide and narrow uprights to the thickness and width given, but leave these pieces ½" or so long for now.

Set up a ¾" wide dado on your table saw and cut a 2¾"-wide × ⅛"-deep channel down the length of each wide upright. Center the channel from side to side.

Reduce the width of the dado to ½" and cut a ½"-wide × ¼"-deep groove down the length of each of the narrow uprights. Glue the narrow uprights into the channels you cut in the wide uprights. Make sure the grooves in the narrow upright are to the inside. Make one end of each glue-up as flush as possible.

Trim the flush ends of the upright assemblies to ensure they are, in fact, flush and square. Tilt the blade on your table saw to 45° and miter the opposite ends, cutting the uprights to length in the process.

Cut the corners off of the plinth and the base as shown in the Base Details. Chuck a 45° chamfer bit in your table-mounted outer and chamfer the top edges of both pieces.

Mark the center of the plinth on its underside, and the center of the base on its topside. Drill 3" diameter holes at these points to create a cavity in which to make the wiring connections. Drill the hole in the plinth deep enough that the thickness of the plinth at the bottom of the hole is only ¼". Make the hole in the base 1" deep.

EIGHT Drilling the 3" diameter holes for the puck lights after the vee assemblies are glued together insures that the holes line up.

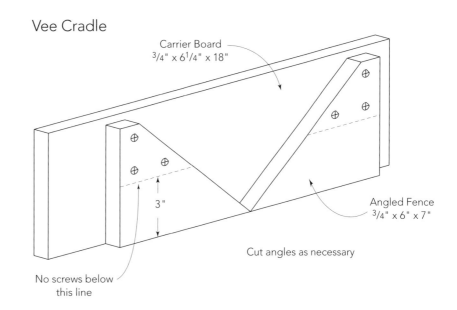

Vee Cradle

Carrier Board
¾" × 6¼" × 18"

Angled Fence
¾" × 6" × 7"

3"

Cut angles as necessary

No screws below this line

Base Details

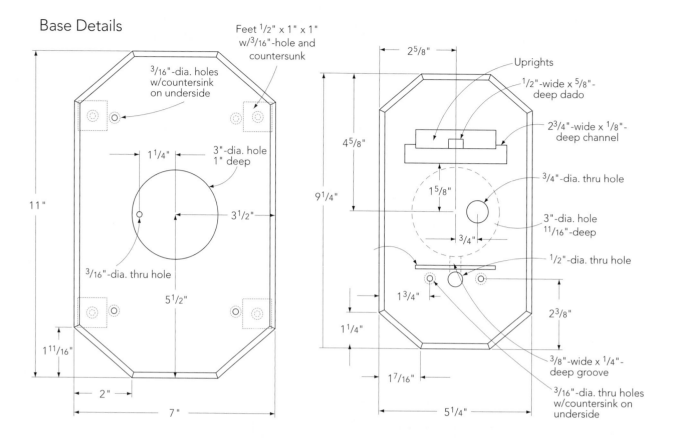

Feet $^1/_2$" x 1" x 1" w/$^3/_{16}$"-hole and countersunk

$^3/_{16}$"-dia. holes w/countersink on underside

$1^1/_4$"

3"-dia. hole 1" deep

11"

$3^1/_2$"

$^3/_{16}$"-dia. thru hole

$5^1/_2$"

$1^{11}/_{16}$"

2"

7"

$2^5/_8$"

Uprights

$^1/_2$"-wide x $^5/_8$"-deep dado

$2^3/_4$"-wide x $^1/_8$"-deep channel

$4^5/_8$"

$^3/_4$"-dia. thru hole

$9^1/_4$"

$1^5/_8$"

3"-dia. hole $^{11}/_{16}$"-deep

$^3/_4$"

$^1/_2$"-dia. thru hole

$1^3/_4$"

$2^3/_8$"

$1^1/_4$"

$^3/_8$"-wide x $^1/_4$"-deep groove

$1^7/_{16}$"

$5^1/_4$"

$^3/_{16}$"-dia. thru holes w/countersink on underside

Draw a centerline across the top-side of the plinth. Measure $1^9/_{16}$" to either side of the centerline and strike lines across to indicate the locations of the uprights. Clamp one of the uprights to the plinth with its inside corner aligned with the layout line and it centered from front to back. Cut biscuit slots in both the plinth and the upright as shown in Photo 9. Repeat the process with the second upright.

Drill the holes in the plinth and base as indicated on the Base Details. Chuck a $^3/_8$" straight bit in your table-mounted router. Rout channels connecting the $^1/_2$" holes at the bottoms of the uprights to the 3" diameter hole you drilled earlier.

Cut the feet to the size specified in the Materials List. Find their centers and drill and countersink them at these points. Glue and screw the feet to the underside of the base.

Finish all the parts before assembling them (unscrew the vee assembly, too). The lamp in the photo is finished with four coats of Minwax Antique Oil finish.

NINE To make the biscuit slots, mark center on the upright. Cut the slot in the plinth with the biscuit joiner's base butted up against the upright. Cut the slot in the upright with the biscuit joiner's base sitting flat on the plinth. In both cases, align the center mark on the joiner with the center mark on the upright.

ASSEMBLY & INSTALLATION

1. Put biscuits in the slots and position the uprights on the plinth, centering them from front to back. Drill pilot holes then screw the uprights in place with 2½" wood screws.

2. Place the lower vee assembly in the cradle formed by the uprights. Drill pilot holes and screw it to the uprights with 1⅝" wood screws.

3. Drill ½" diameter holes at an angle down through the vee assembly into the uprights (see photo). These holes should align with the dadoes in the center of the uprights.

4. Screw the main vee assembly in place.

5. Cut the wires leading from the LED pucks so they are approximately 18" long. Feed the wires down through the uprights and out through the bottom of the plinth. Pop the LEDs free of their bases and screw the bases into the 3" holes. Clip the LEDs back into place.

6. Push the switch down through the ¾" hole in the plinth. You may need to file the hole a little bit to get the switch to fit. Lock the switch in place with the nut it came with.

7. Cut the plug off of the wire that comes out of the transformer. Push the cut end through the hole in the back of the base. Tie a knot in the wire so it can't pull back out of the hole. Leave about 8" of the cut end to work with.

8. Split all three wires into their separate leads. Cut a 12" length of extra wire (from one of the puck wires you cut earlier) and separate it into its two individual leads. Save the one with the long white dashes on the insulation.

9. Strip ¾" of insulation from all the leads (and both ends of the extra piece). Twist the two leads with long white dashes together along with one end of the extra wire. Solder this connection and cap it with a wire nut. Solder the other end of the extra wire to one of the switch terminals.

10. Solder the lead with the long white dashes that comes from the transformer to the other switch terminal. Twist the remaining three leads (all should have text on them) together. Solder this connection and cap it with a wire nut. See Working with LEDs on page 12 for more details. As always, if you don't feel comfortable dealing with the electrical connections, consult with a professional.

11. Coil the wires into the cavity in the plinth. Center the pinth on the the base and screw the pieces together with 2" woodscrews.

12. Place the corner block in the vee. Screw the end mouldings to the main vee pieces to lock the block in place.

Drill ½" holes for the wires down through the lower vee assembly. Position these holes towards the bottom of the 3" hole you drilled earlier. Note: if you look closely, you'll notice a couple things in the photo that don't exactly agree with the text: there is an extra hole in the vee — this was a mistake, and the pieces are unfinished — it makes more sense to finish them prior to assembly, but I wasn't in a position to do that.

A PENDANT FIXTURE COMBINES WITH SOME BENT WOOD TO FORM A COLORFUL TABLE LAMP.
BASE: WALNUT, BENT PIECE: ASH

8 **WILD FLOWER** LAMP

I FOUND THIS GLASS SHADE as I was wandering the lighting aisles of my local home center. I was drawn to the bright color and sleek shape. After looking at it and its cousins (there are a number of different shapes and colors available) I decided it would make a nice table lamp.

What the red thing is, is a glass shade for what is called a mini pendant lamp. Pendant lamps are lighting fixtures meant to dangle from the ceiling by their power cords. Rather than do this, I thought it would be more fun to make a base from which I could suspend the shade. A further search of the lighting section revealed a mini pendant kit containing the light socket and cord. I was glad to find these, as they meant I wouldn't have to invent a means of holding the shade (and the bulb) on my own.

The design itself evolved from a series of sketches. At the time, spring was arriving with its onrush of flowers and leaves. I guess I had these on my mind because the final sketch and design remind me a lot of some flowers I've seen.

As with most lamps, this one has a heavier base attached to a lighter support structure that holds up the lamp parts. The base is turned from thick (16/4) stock although you can easily glue together two or more thinner pieces if you can't find a piece of heavy material. The support is a bent piece made up of thin layers that were glued together over a curved form. This is a process called bent lamination. If you haven't tried bending wood this way, this is a great project with which to start as the bend is fairly gentle and doesn't require much effort to coax into existence.

Fabrication

Cut three pieces of ¾" × 7" × 27¾" MDF, plywood, or particle board to make into the bending form. Draw a 29¼" radius arc on one of the pieces with a trammel as shown in the Form Layout. Cut along the curve on the band saw, then sand the the curve smooth. I usually do this on a stationary belt sander. Use the first piece as a pattern and trace the curve onto the other two pieces. Cut and sand them to shape. Screw the three pieces together and do a final sanding to make the curved edges all even with each other. Once the pieces are screwed together, sketch the cutout areas onto one of the faces and cut away these areas on the band saw.

Cut a piece of 6/4 stock so it is 32" long. Joint and plane it, leaving it as thick as possible — you'll cut the bent pieces to width later. Also joint one edge so it is straight and rip the other edge to make it parallel. Rip a series of strips off the edge of the board for bending as shown in Photo 1. Rather than trying to set the fence for such a narrow cut, set up a stop block to the left of the blade as shown to control the thickness of the strips. I used ash for bends on my lamp. Ash bends very well (as does oak). But the bend here is gentle enough that you can probably use any species of wood. Make a test cut from the material you are using and bend it around your form to see if you have the thickness right. I used pieces that were ³⁄₁₆" thick.

To set the stop (I use the butt end of a feather board), use the rip fence

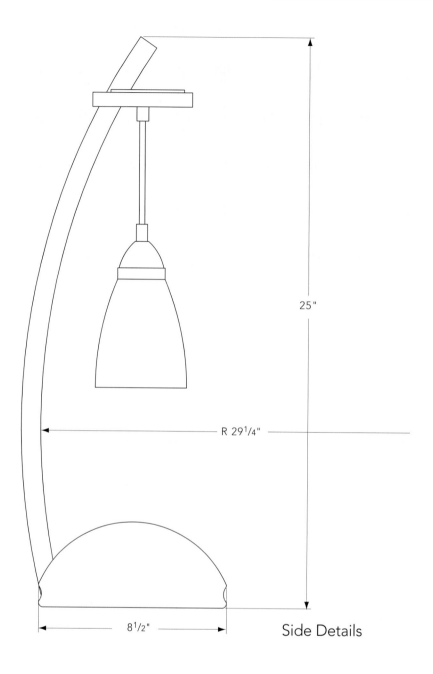

25"

R 29¼"

8½"

Side Details

INCHES (MILLIMETERS)

REFERENCE	QUANTITY	PART	STOCK	THICKNESS	(mm)	WIDTH	(mm)	LENGTH	(mm)
A	5	laminations	ash	³⁄₁₆	(5)	1½	(38)	32	(813)
B	1	base	walnut	3¾	(95)	8½	(216)	8½	(216)
C	1	disk	walnut	⁵⁄₈	(16)	4½	(115)	diameter	
D	1	cap	walnut	⅛	(3)	3⁵⁄₈	(92)	diameter	
E	1	cover plate	walnut	¼	(6)	3	(76)	diameter	

HARDWARE

#6 x 2" Trimhead Wood Screws (2)
#6 x 1¼" Brass Wood Screws (2)
#4 x ½" Brass Wood Screws (3)
#6 x 1" Wood Screws (2)
Mini Pendant Kit
   (Westinghouse #70284)
2¼" Fitter Glass Shade
Lamp Cord w/ thumb switch
wire nuts (2)

Form Layout

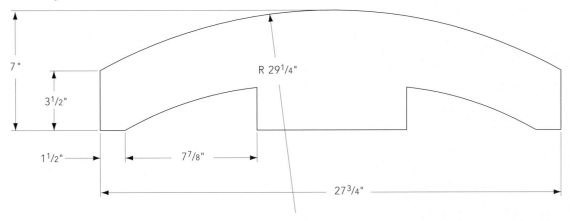

7 "

3¹/₂"

R 29¹/₄"

1¹/₂"

7⁷/₈"

27³/₄"

to position the board so the offcut is the thickness you are after. Adjust the stop so it just kisses the left side of the board an inch or two in front of the blade and lock it in place. Make the first cut. Then adjust the rip fence so the left side of the board just kisses the stop. Make the second cut. Keep going, adjusting the fence after each cut until you have enough strips. For each of the lamps, you'll need nine strips, plus a couple extras to help distribute the clamp pressure.

Spread glue on the first three laminations. Add the fourth piece to the stack along with two extra strips (I made my extras from ¹/₄" plywood) to protect the good pieces from the

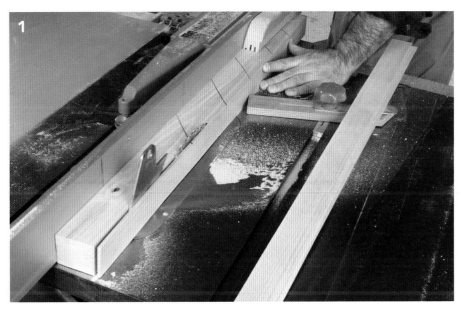

ONE When cutting strips for bent lamination, keeping the pieces in the order they were cut allows you to glue them up so the grain matches. To help keep things straight, draw a series of diagonal lines across the board so you can put them back in order should things get mixed up.

TWO To keep the bent piece from sticking to the form, cover the curved surface with a layer of plastic packing tape before clamping the pieces over it.

THREE Jointing a bent piece is very much like jointing a straight piece. Start with the leading edge against the fence and roll the piece through the cut, trying to maintain contact with the fence right over the cutter head.

FOUR To cut a bent piece, push it past the blade with a sort of a rolling motion, keeping the section being cut in contact with the table right at the front of the blade.

FIVE Guide the bent piece along the fence as you rout the groove for the cord. Like with the table saw cut, roll the piece as you push it past the bit, trying to keep it in contact with the table right where the bit is cutting.

clamps. Bend the stack over the form starting in the middle and working your way out as shown in Photo 2.

Once the glue dries, remove the clamps and scrape away the excess glue. Joint one side of the bent piece to make it straight and square to the convex face as shown in Photo 3.

Once you have established one straight edge, make the second side parallel to it by running the bent piece through the table saw as shown in Photo 4. Set the fence to leave the piece as wide as possible while still cleaning up the rough edge.

Chuck a ⅜" straight bit in your table-mounted router and rout a ¼"-deep groove down the center of the convex side of the bend as shown in Photo 5.

Put the piece back on the form and glue the final two laminations to it. When the glue is dry, joint one side and cut the other on the table saw to clean up the rough edges. Then cut the piece to its final width of 1⅜". Remove material from both sides if necessary to keep the groove centered. Don't worry if the piece is narrower than specified, just adapt the width of the notches in the base and disk to fit.

Cut a piece of wood for the base into a circular shape slightly larger in diameter than is specified in the Materials List. If necessary, face glue two or more thinner pieces to make up the necessary thickness.

Mount the base on a head stock and turn it to the shape shown in the Side View. You may want to use the tailstock to help support the piece while you turn it roughly to size as shown in Photo 6. Sand the base while it is still on the lathe and apply a coat or two of finish. (I used Minwax Antique Oil Finish.)

Set a tee-bevel to 84° and mark one end of the bend as shown in Photo 7. Cut along your layout line on the band saw. Measure 25" from the cut end and make a mark along the outside of the curve. Cut the curve to length at this point. This cut should be more or less square (or as square as you can make something along a curved line.)

Lay out a radius line on the bottom of the base as shown in Photo 8. Layout two additional lines parallel to the radius line and $^{11}/_{16}$" on either side of it. When working with dark woods such

SIX The exact shape of the base isn't critical, although it should be relatively heavy to help keep the lamp upright. Here I have the tailstock in position to provide a little added support as I rough the piece to its general shape.

SEVEN To lay out the initial cut on the curve, set a tee-bevel for 84 degrees and hold it along the inside of the curve. While the angle you mark may be somewhat different from that I marked, it will be close enough.

EIGHT Draw a radius line from the center of the base out to the rim. Then add two lines parallel to the first. Each of these lines should be parallel to the radius line and $^{11}/_{16}$" on either side. Double check to make sure the lines are $1^{3}/_{8}$" apart.

as walnut, I often will attach a layer of masking tape on which to make my layout marks.

Lay out a perpendicular line between the lines you drew that were parallel to the radius line. This line should be in from the edge of the base a distance equal to the thickness of the bent piece. Saw along the parallel lines as shown in Photo 9.

Remove the waste between the cuts with a chisel as shown in Photo 10. Try the bent piece in the notch and adjust the notch's angle until the bottom of the bent piece (the end you cut at an 84° angle) seems to be parallel to the bottom of the base.

Cut a piece of stock for the top disk to the size listed in the Materials List. Cut it round on the band saw and cut a notch in it for the bent piece. Like the notch in the base, the bottom of the notch in the base is angled. Again, the exact angle may vary, but it will be about 120°. The important thing is that the disk ends up parallel to the ground. The approximate size of the notch is shown in the Disk Detail.

Base Section View

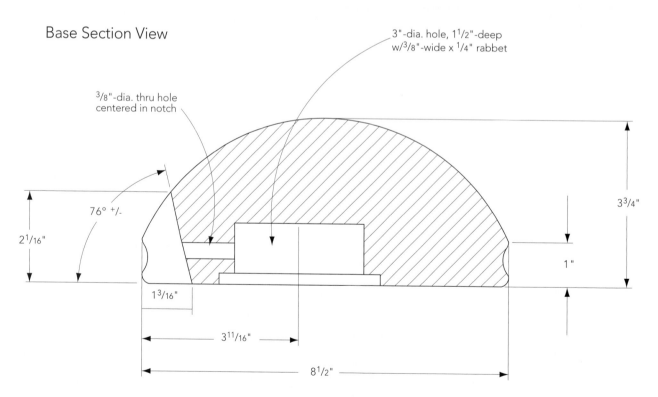

3"-dia. hole, 1 1/2"-deep w/3/8"-wide x 1/4" rabbet

3/8"-dia. thru hole centered in notch

76° +/-

2 1/16"

3 3/4"

1"

1 3/16"

3 11/16"

8 1/2"

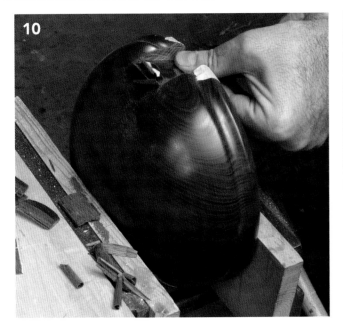

Once the you have the disk fit to the bent piece, trace its location on the bent piece's sides and across its front. Use these lines as guides as you cut a ⅛" deep notch in the bent piece to help keep the disk in place as shown in Photo 11.

Drill a ¹³⁄₃₂" hole through the center of the disk. Counterbore this hole with a 1" diameter Forstner bit, leaving the disk about ⅛" thick at the bottom of the counter bore. Drill a ½" hole that starts in the notch and intersects with the counterbore as shown in Photo 12.

TEN With so many curves to deal with, you have to work a little more intuitively, fitting pieces together so they look right rather than relying on hard measurements. The important thing about attaching the bent piece to the base is getting the bent piece to be perpendicular to the table top when viewed from the front.

ELEVEN When you make the cuts for the notch in the bent piece, note that they should be angled to match the lines you traced from the disk.

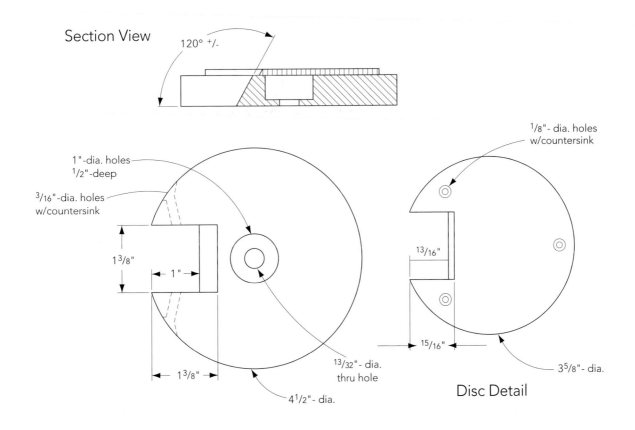

Section View

120° ⁺/⁻

1"-dia. holes
½"-deep

³⁄₁₆"-dia. holes
w/countersink

1 ³⁄₈"

1"

1 ³⁄₈"

4½"- dia.

¹³⁄₃₂"- dia.
thru hole

⅛"- dia. holes
w/countersink

13/16"

15/16"

3⅝"- dia.

Disc Detail

Drill a matching hole in the bent piece so the wires can get into the groove you routed earlier.

Ease the edges of the cap with a ⅛" roundover bit chucked in a table-mounted router.

Cut a piece of ⅛"-thick material for the cap. Cut it round on the band saw and notch it to fit around the bent piece. Drill and countersink three holes for the short screws that will hold it in place atop the disk.

Drill a 2¼"-diameter × 1½"-deep hole in the bottom of the base. Locate the hole as shown in the Base Section View. Chuck a ⅜" rabbeting bit in your table-mounted router and cut a ¼"-deep rabbet around the edge of the hole.

Drill a ½"-diameter hole in the concave face of the bent piece so you can get the wires out of the groove. Center it from side-to-side and locate it 1" up from the lower end of the piece. Drill a corresponding hole in the center of the notch in the base leading into the 2¼" hole you drilled earlier.

Cut a piece of ¼" material into a 3" diameter circle to serve as a cover for the wiring. Fit it carefully into the rabbet, then drill both pieces for the screws that will hold it in place as shown in Photo 13. Drill a ¼" hole through the center of the plate for the power cord.

TWELVE As you drill the hole in the disk for the wires to pass through, grip the disk with a wooden hand screw. The clamp makes the piece easier to hold onto, and it helps ensure the hole is properly aligned.

THIRTEEN I found a piece of Styrofoam packing material that makes a great holder for the base when I have to work on its underside. Try to be a little smarter than I was and offset the screw from the hole you drilled for the wires to come through.

Drill two ³⁄₁₆" holes through the bent piece for the two screws that attach it to the base. Locate these screw holes on either side of the ½" hole you drilled for the wires and counterbore them for plugs with a ¼" bit.

Cut a plug to fill the hole where the groove comes out the top of the bent piece. Glue it in place and sand it flush, gently rounding the end of the bent piece in the process.

Temporarily assemble the pieces, screwing the bent piece to the base and the disk to the bent piece as shown in Photo 14.

Disassemble the lamp and finish all the pieces. I finished the lamp in the photo with several coats of Minwax Antique Oil Finish, a wiping varnish.

14

FOURTEEN Prior to finishing, put all the pieces together to make sure everything fits as it should. Double check that the bent piece is perpendicular to the table when viewed from the front.

ASSEMBLY

1. The pendent kit comes with a wire that runs from the socket up through a dish-like metal fitting that is meant to go against the ceiling. You won't be needing this fitting, but you will need some of the hardware that is attached to it. Loosen the set screw that holds the wire in the collar in the center of the fitting and pull the wire free. Also undo the nut that holds the collar to the fitting. Hang on to the collar , the hex nut, the washer, and the nipple that everything is threaded onto.

2. Push the nipple up through the hole in the center of the disk until the collar butts up against the disks underside. Fasten it in place with the washer and the hex nut. Feed the wire from the fixture up through the collar until the fixture is hanging about 4" below the disk. Tighten the set screw to lock the wire in place.

3. Strip the heavy plastic tubing off so you are left with the three individual wires. Be careful not to cut the insulation on the wires. Exam the wires carefully. You'll find one has a green stripe, one has a white stripe and one has no stripe on its insulation. Clip the wire with the green stripe off near where it comes out of the nipple. This is a ground wire and won't be necessary for a table lamp.

4. Push the two remaining wires through the hole that leads to the notch. Then feed them into the bent piece and push them down until you can fish them out the hole in at the bottom. From here, push the wires through the hole that leads from the notch into the 2¼" hole.

5. Work the slack out of the wire and screw the disk to the bent piece and the bent piece to the base.

6. Cut the excess wire, leaving your self about 8" of wire to make the connections. Push the end of the lamp cord up through the hole in the cover plate and tie it in a knot so it can't pull back through.

7. Strip about ¾" of insulation off the ends of the individual wires. Twist the lead with the white stripe together with the ribbed lead on the lamp cord. Twist the other two leads together as well. Cap the connections with wire nuts. Coil the Wires into the 2¼" hole and screw the cover plate in place.

8. Attach three feet to the underside of the base. Plug the holes in the bottom of the bent piece and sand the plugs flush. Wipe some finish over the plugs to blend them in with the rest of the piece. For more details of making the electrical connections, see page 8. As always, if you are not sure how to do the wiring, consult with a professional.

EVEN IF YOU LIVE FAR FROM THE COAST, THE LAMP WILL SERVE AS A BEACON OF HOME. WITH BOTH A REGULAR LAMP SOCKET AND AN ENCLOSED LED PUCK, YOU'LL HAVE A CHOICE OF GENERAL ILLUMINATION, OR A MORE INTIMATE, SOFT GLOW. **CHERRY, GLASS**

9 LIGHTHOUSE LAMP

IN CONTRAST TO THE TALL, cylindrical lighthouses that mark the U.S. coast along the Atlantic Ocean, the polygonal lighthouses of the Chesapeake Bay tend to be somewhat squatter in stature. This is not to say that they are lacking in charm, just that they present a somewhat different edifice to the world. When I saw this six-sided glass "Hedron" block in Home Depot, it immediately reminded me of these inland nautical sentinels and I knew I wanted to use it in a lamp.

After toting the block back to my studio, it took a little puzzling to figure out just how to make this lamp work. My first thought was to enclose the block in some kind of framework that would connect the upper part to the base. But after sketching a few possibilities, it became obvious that block was made so nicely, adding an external frame was superfluous. But there was still the question of how to connect everything together. A little internet research revealed that it was quite possible to drill holes in glass block provided one has the right drill bit. A stop at my local hardware store took care of this shortage. After drilling four 1/2" holes in the block with my new bit, I was able to run lengths of lamp rod up through the center of the block, sandwiching it between the two pieces of wood that make up the upper and lower parts. The lamp rod also solved the problem of how to run the wires for the main light — a compact fluorescent bulb in a standard light socket.

As with the other lights in this book that make use of glass block, the block itself is lit from below with an LED "puck" light. These low voltage light fixtures work well in this situation because they provide a nice soft glow appropriate for a night light without getting very hot. They also last a long time. My only regret with setup is that the lamp has two power cords — one for the main light and the other (low voltage) for the LED.

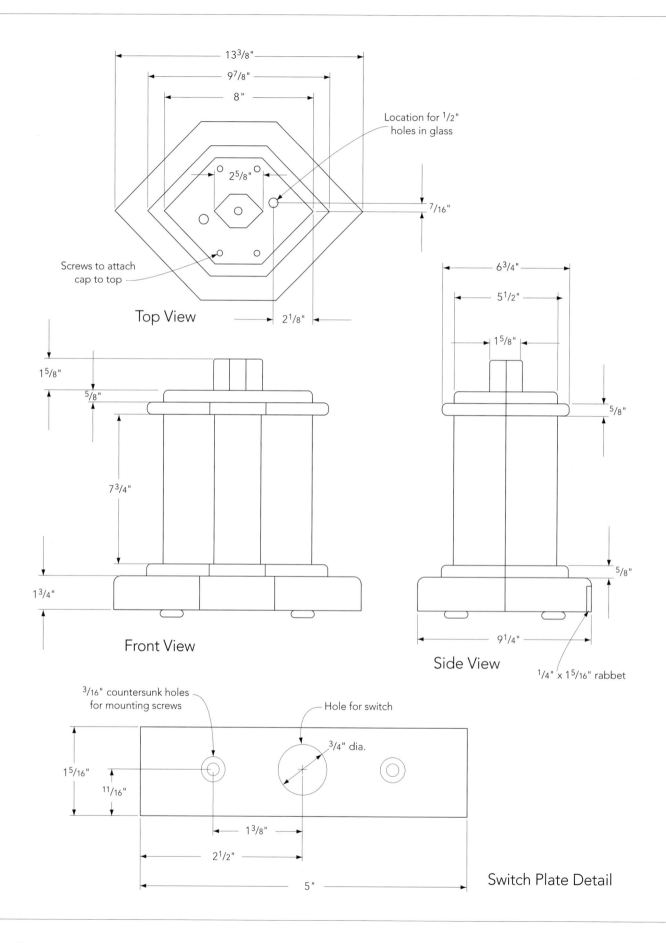

Top View

Front View

Side View

Switch Plate Detail

INCHES (MILLIMETERS)

REFERENCE	QUANTITY	PART	STOCK	THICKNESS	(mm)	WIDTH	(mm)	LENGTH	(mm)	COMMENTS
A	2	top/bottom	cherry	5/8	(16)	6 3/4	(171)	9 7/8	(251)	
B	1	cap	cherry	5/8	(16)	5 1/2	(140)	8	(203)	
C	1	base	cherry	1 3/4	(45)	9 1/4	(235)	13 3/8	(340)	
D	1	cover plate	cherry	1/4	(6)	2	(51)	4 1/4	(108)	
E	1	switch plate	cherry	1/4	(6)	1 5/16	(33)	5	(127)	
F	1	riser	cherry	1 5/8	(41)	1 5/8	(45)	2 5/8	(67)	

HARDWARE

Hedron Glass Block (Pittsburgh Corning)
1/8 IP x 9" nipples (2)
1/8" IP x 2 1/4" nipple
1/8" IP hex nuts (8)
#8 x 1 1/4" Wood Screws (8)
#8 x 1 5/8" Wood Screws (6)

LED Puck Light Kit (Hampton Bay #957 245)
SPST Rocker Switch (Radio Shack #275-0693)
Bottom Clamp
Lamp Socket w/ Switch
Lamp Cord
Feet (4) (Woodcraft #50S41)

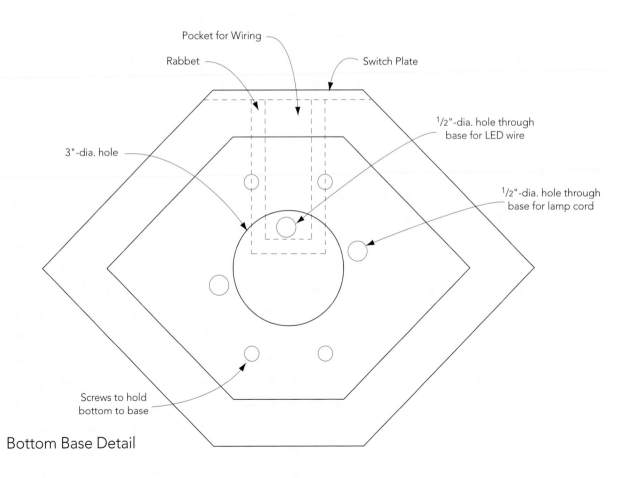

Pocket for Wiring

Rabbet

Switch Plate

1/2"-dia. hole through base for LED wire

3"-dia. hole

1/2"-dia. hole through base for lamp cord

Screws to hold bottom to base

Bottom Base Detail

Fabrication

Trace the shape of the glass block onto a piece of ½" MDF. Carefully cut along the lines to create a pattern. Locate the two holes for the lamp rod on the pattern as shown in the Top View. Drill these holes with a ½" bit on the drill press. Note, the holes are offset from the center line of the block because this block has a seam that runs along the center line that would be difficult to drill through.

Use the pattern to locate the holes on the block. Put pieces of masking tape on the block so you can mark it. Drill the four holes through the block with a ½" carbide-tipped glass drill bit as shown in Photo 1. Fill a squirt bottle with water and keep the bit and glass wet to keep things from getting too hot.

Cut the top, bottom and cap to the sizes specified in the Materials List. Trace around the pattern to lay out the shape of the cap. Center the pattern on the top and bottom pieces and mark the holes. Also trace around the pattern to begin the layouts for these pieces.

Draw another set of lines on the top and bottom pieces ⅝" outside the lines from the pattern. Carefully cut along these lines on the table saw. Use a miter gauge to guide the pieces past the blade as shown in Photo 2. Cut the cap to shape with the same set up.

Drill the holes through the top and bottom with a ¹³⁄₃₂" bit. Also drill a ¹³⁄₃₂" hole through the center of the cap. Drill ⅛"-deep × ¾"-diameter counterbores on both sides of the holes in the bottom and on the top side of the holes in the top. Drill a similar counterbore in the underside of the cap, but make it ⁵⁄₁₆" deep.

Use the pattern to mark one of the hole locations on the underside of the cap. As you face the lamp, this will be the right-hand hole. Drill a ½"-diameter hole at this location, approximately ⅜" deep.

Rout a ⁵⁄₁₆"-wide × ¼"-deep groove that runs from the hole you just drilled to the center counterbore in the underside of the cap as shown in Photo 3.

Round over the top edges of the bottom piece and the cap, and both the

ONE When drilling glass, excess heat will both harm the bit and possibly cause the glass to crack. To keep things cool, squirt the operation with water as you work. The block is surprisingly easy to drill. Cleaning up the white, powdery residue is probably the biggest nuisance. I had to rinse my block out several times to get it clean.

TWO After tracing the pattern, you should have four cuts to make to cut the top and bottom pieces to the right shape. Make these cuts on the table saw with the miter gauge set at 45° to the blade.

3

top and bottom edges of the top piece with a ¼" roundover bit in a table-mounted router.

Cut the base to the size indicated in the Materials List. You may need to edge glue some narrower pieces to make up the full width. Center the pattern on the piece and trace around it. Make a second set of lines, 1⅞" outside the tracing, to complete the layout.

Mark the center of the base and drill a shallow (³⁄₁₆") 3"-diameter hole there. Also mark the center of the bottom piece and drill a 3"-diameter hole through it. Drill and countersink four holes through the bottom so you can fasten it to the base as shown in the Bottom/Base Detail.

Temporarily screw the bottom to the base, aligning the pieces both with the big hole in the center and making sure the edges of the bottom are parallel to the layout lines on the base. Note: As you align the pieces, orient each board so the better-looking grain is towards the front. Mark the location of the right-hand hole on the base. Un-screw the bottom and set it aside.

Drill a ½" hole through the base at the mark you just made. Also drill a ½" hole through the base near the back of the 3" hole. The main power cord will come up through the right-hand hole, while wire for the LED light will come up through the other.

Turn the base over and lay out a rectangular pocket to contain the connections for the LED. Center the pocket from end to end. Make it 1¼" wide, about 3⅞" long and 1⁵⁄₁₆" deep. Rout the pocket

THREE The wire that comes up through one of the rods in the glass block needs a channel to get to the hole in the center of the cap. I cut this channel with a ⁵⁄₁₆" straight bit in a hand held router. Clamp the cap to your bench and make the cut in two shallow passes. It doesn't have to be perfect, so I opted to do this freehand.

with a ⅝" straight bit in a hand-held router. Guide the router against a straightedge and make the cut in several passes. Shift the fence and repeat the process to make the cut wider. You will be routing into one of the ½" holes you drilled earlier. This is supposed to happen.

Rabbet the edges of the pocket, making the cut ⅜" wide and ¼" deep. I used the same straight bit I had in the router from the previous step, but you could also use a rabbeting bit with a guide bearing. Square the corners of the rabbet with a chisel as shown in Photo 4.

Set up a ¼"-wide dado blade on your table saw and set the depth of cut to 1⁵⁄₁₆". Use this set up to cut a ¼"-deep × 1⁵⁄₁₆"-wide dado along the back edge of the base as shown in the Side View. This rab-bet will run across the pocket you routed earlier.

Cut a strip of ¼" thick material and then cut both a cover plate and switch plate from it. The cover plate should fit in the rabbet you routed in the underside of the base, and the switch plate in the rabbet along the back edge. The switch plate is specified with

4

some extra length — you'll trim it to size as you cut the base to shape later. Drill a ¾" hole through the switch plate as shown in the Switch Plate Detail. Drill and countersink two screw holes through the piece as indicated. Screw the plate to the base, centering the ¾" hole on the routed pocket.

Cut the corners off the base, cutting it to shape as you did with the top, bottom, and cap. Double check your set-up to make sure you will not be cutting into the screws holding the switch plate, however, leave the plate in place. This operation will trim it to the right size and shape. Round over the top edges of the base with a ⅜" roundover bit.

Cut the riser to the size given in the Materials List. Cut off its corners at 45° to make its shape match that of the other pieces. I found this piece too small to hold safely on the table saw, so I made the cuts on the band saw and then sanded it to final size.

Drill a ¹³⁄₃₂" hole through center of the riser. Drill a ³⁄₁₆" deep × ¾" diameter counterbore from the underside of the piece.

Round over the top edges of the riser. Again, I found the piece too small to run on the router table, so I made these roundovers with a block plane followed by sandpaper. Aim for about a ⅛" radius.

Drill and countersink four holes in the cap as shown in the Top View. These are for the screws that attach the cap to the top. Also drill and countersink two holes from the underside of the cap for

FOUR You can leave the pocket itself with a scalloped end, but the rabbet needs to be square.

TIP When drilling small pieces on a drill press, grip them with a wooden handscrew. This makes them much easier to hold and makes the operation a lot safer to boot.

attaching the riser. Slide a nipple through the hole in the riser and use it to center the riser on the cap. Check to make sure the edges of both pieces are parallel, then clamp them together. Drill pilot holes and screw the cap to the riser.

Finish the four parts of the lamp separately. I finished the lamp in the photo with several coats of Waterlox transparent, a wiping varnish. I also chose to paint the feet to give the lamp a little touch of whimsy. Paint the four feet then screw them to the underside of the base with 1¼" wood screws. Note: the "feet" are actually wooden wheels used on the flat. Countersink the axle holes so the screw heads don't protrude and mar the surface the lamp is resting upon.

ASSEMBLY & INSTALLATION

1. Thread a hex nut onto each of the 9" nipples and spin the nuts so they each are about ³⁄₄" along the length of their pipes. Insert these ends of the nipples into the holes in the bottom. Thread a second nut onto each nipple. Tighten the nuts to lock the nipple in place with its bottom end flush with the underside of the bottom piece.

2. Screw the bottom to the base with 1⁵⁄₈" wood screws. Feed the wire from the LED puck down through the hole in the base and fit the puck itself into the 3" opening. There is no need to screw it in place, it is not going anywhere. Slide the glass block over the nipples to rest on the bottom as shown below. Set the top in place and hold it there with nuts tightened on the nipples.

3. Slide the 2¼" nipple through the cap/riser assembly and nut it in place, capturing the bottom clamp in the process. Feed the lamp cord up through the right-hand nipple. When it comes out the top, feed it through the cap/riser as well. Center the cap on the top and screw it in place, taking care to capture the cord in the groove.

4. Thread the bottom part of a lamp socket on the to nipple. Wire the cord to the socket as discussed on page 8. If you are not comfortable making the electrical connections, consult with a licensed electrician.

5. Remove the switch plate from the back of the lamp. Slide the switch in place and fasten it with its included nut. Cut the wire coming from the LED short — to about 7"- 8" or so. Also clip the connector off of the lead coming from the transformer. Drill a ³⁄₁₆" hole through the center of the cover plate and feed the transformer wire up through it. Tie a knot so the wire can't pull back through the hole. Leave about 7"- 8" of wire past the knot.

6. Separate the conductors on each of the wires so you have four separate leads. Notice that on each pair, one lead has lettering on the insulation, while the other just has a series of lines. Strip about ½" of insulation off of the ends of the lettered leads. Twist these ends together, solder the connection, and twist on a wire nut. Make sure the nut covers all exposed metal. Strip the insulation on the other two leads and solder them to the switch terminals.

7. Re-attach the switch plate to the base. Fold the wires into the pocket and screw the cover plate in place. Take the lamp along when you go shopping for a shade.

Assembly is mostly a matter of stacking all the piece one on top of the next and joining them with various fasteners.

LAMPS ARE CLASSIC LATHE PROJECTS AND OFFER A GOOD WAY TO BE EITHER A TURNER TURNED LAMPMAKER, OR A LAMPMAKER TURNED TURNER. **WALNUT**

10 **TURNED** LAMP

IF YOU HAVE ACCESS TO A LATHE, the possibilities for lamps are virtually unlimited. With a little heavy stock and some imagination, you can "turn" out a lamp in as little as an hour or two. The inspiration for this particular design came from a lamp my father made forty or fifty years ago that is still lighting their home today. It has a simple, yet elegant form that really gives it a timeless appeal.

I made my lamp from walnut, but any hardwood will work. Heavier woods tend to be a little better as the added weight helps to keep the lamp from being too tippy. If you find your lamp is somewhat top-heavy, you can always add a larger diameter base to the bottom.

From a technical standpoint, the most difficult task is drilling the hole through the center of the piece. On a trip to my local homecenter, I took a look at their drill bit collection and saw several long bits that will help you with this chore. With a full-sized lathe, you can usually hold the bit in a chuck mounted in the tailstock.

INCHES (MILLIMETERS)

REFERENCE	QUANTITY	PART	STOCK	THICKNESS	(mm)	WIDTH	(mm)	
A	1	base	walnut	3¹/₂	(95)	12³/₈	(315)	dia.

HARDWARE

¹/₈ IP x 2¹/₂" nipple
Bottom Clamp
¹/₈ IP nut
Socket w/ switch
lamp cord

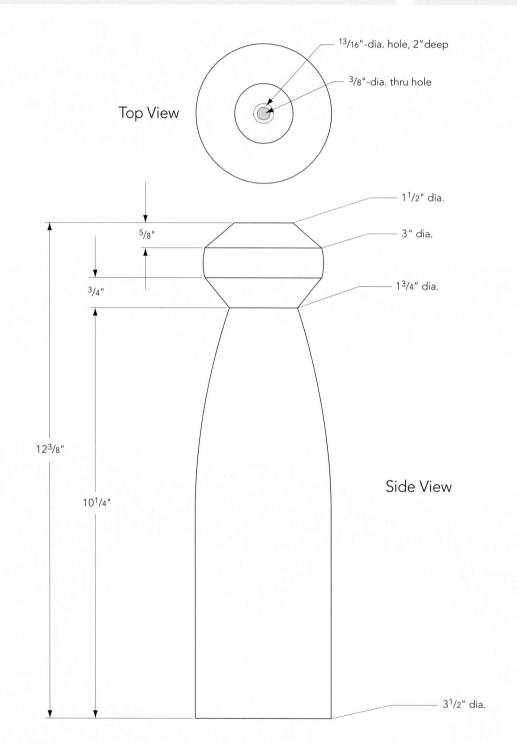

Top View

¹³/₁₆"-dia. hole, 2"deep

³/₈"-dia. thru hole

1¹/₂" dia.

3 " dia.

5/₈"

1³/₄" dia.

3/₄"

12³/₈"

10¹/₄"

Side View

3¹/₂" dia.

Fabrication

Cut a blank for the lamp to the size specified in the Materials List. If possible, try to find a piece of 16/4 so you can make the lamp from a single piece. If not, face glue thinner pieces together to make up the thickness required.

Draw diagonals from corner to corner across both ends of the piece to determine where the centers are.

Cut the corners off the blank with the blade on your table saw tilted over to 45°. Don't worry about making the piece a perfect octagon. You're just trying to remove some of the excess material to make turning a little easier.

Screw a small face plate to one end of the blank, centering it as well as possible. Mount the blank on your lathe and support the other end with a live center in the tail stock as shown in Photo 1. Turn the blank round, then turn it to shape. Sand away the tool marks.

Once you have the blank turned and sanded, mount a Jacobs chuck in the tail stock. Drill a $13/32$"-diameter hole into the end of the base, 2" deep as shown in photo 2. This creates a hole the nipple will fit into. Swap the bigger bit for a $3/8$" hanger bit and drill a hole through the length of the base. Back the bit out of the hole every few inches to clear the chips and prevent heat build up.

Do any final sanding and apply the first coat of finish while the base is still on the lathe. I used a wiping varnish, but feel free to use your own favorite. After the finish dries, remove the base from the lathe. Drill a $5/16$"-diameter hole for the cord about $3/8$" up from the bottom in the least attractive side of the base, making it the back. Drill the hole so it intersects with the hole you drilled down through the center.

ASSEMBLY & INSTALLATION

1. Apply several more coats of finish, rubbing out and polishing as need be.
2. When you are happy with the finish, epoxy a $1/8$" IP x $2^1/2$" nipple in the hole. Try not to get any epoxy on the exposed threads. Also try not to get epoxy inside the pipe. If this happens, however, don't worry. You can always run a drill bit through the pipe after the epoxy sets.
3. Slip a bottom clamp onto the pipe and hold it in place with a hex nut. Thread the base of a lamp socket onto the pipe. Run a two-conductor wire through the hole in the back of the base and up through the pipe. Attach the wires to the business part of the lamp socket as described in the Introduction.

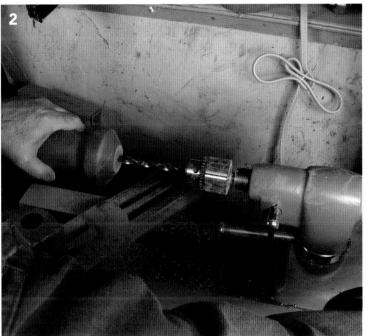

ONE I did most of the turning with a fairly big gouge, then finished up with a skew. Turn the piece round first, then start working it to the shape shown in the Side View. Stop the lathe periodically and run your hands over the curves to make sure they are fair (without dips and lumps). If you have trouble cutting smooth curves with your chisels, don't fret. You can always refine them with course sand paper.

TWO When drilling a hole on the lathe, the bit serves as the center in the tail stock. Butt it up against the workpiece before starting the machine.

WHILE THE WOODEN SHADE ISN'T TRANSLUCENT LIKE A PAPER SHADE, THE SLITS CUT THROUGH ITS PANELS ALLOW A SURPRISING AMOUNT OF LIGHT THROUGH. **DYED MAPLE, BIRCH PLYWOOD**

WOODEN SHADE LAMP

AS I'VE GONE THROUGH THE PROCESS of putting this book together, one of the shapes I've come back to several times is the truncated pyramid — essentially a square-in-cross-section solid that tapers from big at one end to smaller at the other. While the name doesn't do a lot for me, I find the form itself really quite pleasing. This lamp makes use of three of these TPs — one for the base, one for the stem and a final one for the shade.

In many ways, it is the shade that makes this lamp unique. Rather than building a lamp with the thought that I might find a nice commercial shade to go with it, I decided to try and make all of the parts (excluding the electrics) myself. This proved to be an interesting challenge. When you make a shade from an opaque material, such as wood, you are either limited to the light that is thrown up and down from the bulb, or you need to find a way to allow light to come through the material itself. This is the approach I took. After playing with a number of variations, I arrived at the design shown here. It features a number of slits that pierce each of the shade's panels allowing the lamp to throw light to the sides as well as up and down.

The slits follow the angled sides of the shade panels and form sort of a chevron pattern. I made the cuts with a router fitted with a ⅛" straight bit and took care to start and stop them very precisely so as not to detract from the geometric perfection of the design. The corners of the shade are laced together much like the way you would lace up a shoe. The holes for the laces allow a certain amount of light through, added to the overall effect.

The lamp's base is dyed with TransTint wood dye. I had originally thought I would dye the shade as well, but once I had the base made and finished, the shade seemed to want to remain natural.

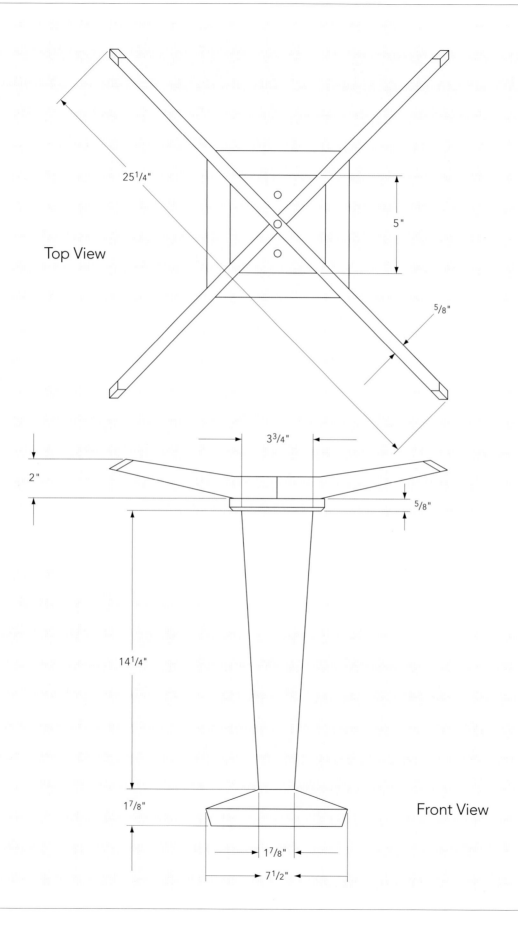

Top View

$25^1/4$"

5 "

$5/8$"

$3^3/4$"

2 "

$5/8$"

$14^1/4$"

Front View

$1^7/8$"

$1^7/8$"

$7^1/2$"

INCHES (MILLIMETERS)

REFERENCE	QUANTITY	PART	STOCK	THICKNESS	(mm)	WIDTH	(mm)	LENGTH	(mm)
A	2	upright halves	maple	$1^7/_8$	(49)	$3^3/_4$	(95)	16	(406)
B	1	base moulding	maple	$1^7/_8$	(49)	3	(76)	34	(864)
C	1	top	maple	$5/_8$	(16)	5	(127)	5	(127)
D	2	arms	maple	$5/_8$	(16)	2	(51)	$25^1/_4$	(641)
E	4	shade quarters	birch ply	$1/_8$	(3)	11	(279)	18	(457)

HARDWARE

#8 x $2^1/_2$" Wood Screws (2)

#8 x $1^1/_2$" Wood Screws (4)

Waxed Linen Thread
(Dick Blick #63012-8234)

Velcro Tape

$1/_8$ IP x $2^1/_2$" Nipple

$1/_8$ IP Hex Nuts (2)

Lamp Socket w/ Switch

Lamp Cord

Fabrication

Mill the two upright halves to the thickness given in the Materials List, but leave the pieces ¼" wider and longer than specified. Chuck a ½" roundnose bit in your table-mounted router and set it to make a cut ¼" deep. Rout a rounded groove down the center of one face of each piece. Glue the two halves together, face to face, with the grooves aligned.

After the glue dries, joint the piece so that it is square. At this point, square is more important than the exact dimensions, but try to keep the piece as close to 3¾" × 3¾" as possible. Cut the piece to its final length.

Set up a ¾"-wide dado on your table saw and cut a 1¾"-square × 1¾"-long tenon on one end of the piece. Guide the piece past the dado head with the miter gauge and use a stop to help control the length of the tenon. Adjust the height of the blade to control the width and thickness of the tenon.

Taper all four sides of the upright on the jointer. This isn't as hairy a procedure as it might seem at first. Lay out the tapers on one face as shown in the Front View. Set the infeed table to make a ¹⁄₁₆"-deep cut. Clamp a stop block to the infeed table so that when you have the upright butted against it, the upright's leading end drops just past the knives onto the outfeed table as shown in Photo 1. Make multiple passes until you reach your layout line. Repeat on the opposite side, making an equal number of passes. Lay out the taper on one of the freshly cut faces and the repeat the process, tapering the two remaining sides. Remove the stop block and give each side a final pass to clean up the the lumps and bumps.

Cut the stock for the base moulding to the size specified in the Materials List. You'll need a total of 34" of moulding, but you can easily make two 17" pieces if that works better with your stock. Tilt the blade on your saw over to a 73° angle and cut the bevel as shown in Photo 2 and in the Moulding Profile Detail

Miter cut both ends of the moulding at 45° to cut the pieces to length. Clamp them down to your bench

ONE Swing the guard out of the way and lower the upright onto the cutter head. Because the leading edge starts on the outfeed table, the knives will just barely kiss the surface. As you feed the piece across the cutter head, the cut will get progressively deeper. Taper two opposing sides first, then make a second layout and repeat the process on the remaining two sides.

TWO This bevel cut is about as deep a cut as a 10" saw can make. If you find your saw straining, lower the blade and make the cut in several passes.

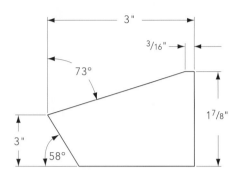

Moulding Profile Detail

and cut mating biscuit slots in the miter faces as shown in Photo 3.

Glue the base up two pieces at a time. Cut custom clamping blocks that allow you to put pressure perpendicular to the glue line as shown in Photo 4.

Once you have the two halves of the base together, trim the mating surfaces on the table saw. Make a vee cut in a scrap of sheet stock to stabilize the pieces as you cut them as shown in Photo 5.

THREE Holding small pieces securely can be a little tricky when cutting the slots for a biscuit joint. Note, if you look closely you'll notice I made the second bevel cut on the moulding before cutting the slots. This was a big mistake. It made the pieces much more difficult to deal with. Make these cuts AFTER you glue the base together.

FOUR When dealing with mitered frames, it is often easier to glue them up is sections. Here, I've cut custom clamping blocks from scrap that allow me to put pressure right where I need it.

FIVE One of the advantages of gluing up the base in sections is that your miters don't have to be 100% perfect. By trimming the halves after they're glued up, you'll be able to correct any slight errors. Cut both halves with the same saw setting to keep them symmetrical.

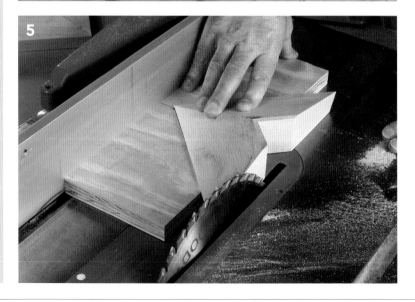

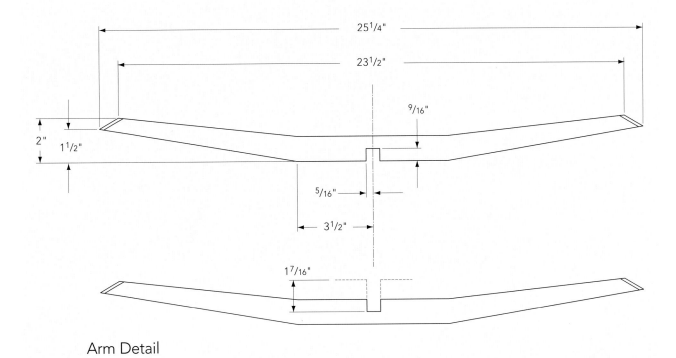

Arm Detail

Make a second vee board similar to the one you used to trim the pieces. Use these two boards as clamping blocks when you glue the halves together.

Make the second bevel cut on all four sides of the base. Tilt the blade to a 58° angle and make the cuts by guiding the base along the fence.

Trim the tenon on the end of the upright to a snug fit in the "mortise" created in the center of the base. I used both a chisel and a rabbet plane to pare the tenon down to size. Glue the upright to the base.

Pick one side of the base to be the back. Cut a ⅜"-wide × ⅜"-deep groove in the center of this piece as a channel for the cord to run in. Make the cut with a ⅜" straight bit in your table-mounted router. Guide the base along the fence and stop the cut when it reaches the hole in the center of the upright.

Cut the top and the arms to the sizes specified in the Materials List. Drill a ¹³/₃₂" hole through the center of the top. Counterbore the hole from the underside with a ¾" Forstner bit. Make the counterbore ¼" deep. Also chamfer the top's lower edges with a 45° chamfer bit in your table-mounted router.

Set up a ⅝"-wide dado blade on your table saw. Cut mating notches at the centers of both arms as shown in the Arm Detail. Note that depths of the notches are not equal due to the ultimate shape of the arms.

Cut the arms to shape on the band saw. Scrape, plane, and sand away the saw marks. Temporarily put the arms together and drill a ¹³/₃₂" hole down through the center of the joint.

Drill the top for the screws that will hold down the arms, and for the screws that hold the top to the upright as shown in the Top Detail.

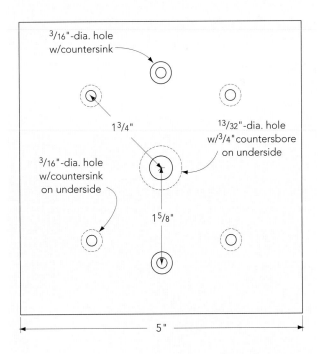

Top Detail

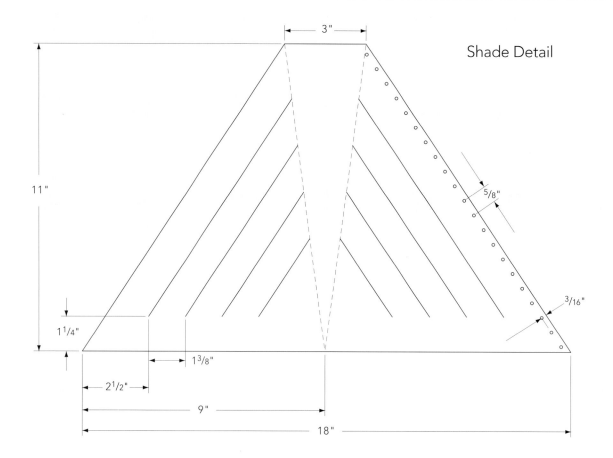

Shade Detail

3"

11"

5/8"

3/16"

1 1/4"

1 3/8"

2 1/2"

9"

18"

Cut the plywood for the shade quarters to the shape shown in the Shade Detail. Rip the plywood to width on your table saw. Then make the angled cuts, guiding the piece with the miter gauge.

Drill the holes along the edges of the pieces on the drill press. Put a fresh scrap on the table to drill into to minimize tear out and drill the pieces with the good side up. Position a fence behind the bit to help keep the holes a uniform distance from the edge.

Lay out the slots on each of the shade quarters as indicated in the Shade Detail. Drill ⁷⁄₆₄" holes at the beginning and ending point of each line. Chuck an ⅛" straight bit in a hand-held router (I used a laminate trimmer) and attach a ⅜" guide bushing to the base. Put a piece of scrap MDF on your bench so you don't rout into the bench's surface. Fasten the shade quarter to the MDF with double-sided tape. Clamp a straightedge across the quarter parallel to one of your

SIX The tricky part about cutting the lines in the shade is starting and stopping the router at the right spots. By drilling a slightly smaller hole at either ends of the lines, I found I could carefully tip the router in to start the cut, and stop it with a minimum of fuss.

layout lines, but ³⁄₁₆" offset from it. If necessary, use one of the other quarters to help support the straight-edge. Guide the router along the straightedge to make the cut as shown in Photo 6.

Stitch together the shade corners as shown in Photo 7. Place the laced-up shade on top of the the arms and center it. Sketch the angles formed by the shade onto the arm ends and use a chisel to bevel the ends as shown in Photo 8. Attach Velcro tape to the ends of the arms and the inside of the shade to hold the shade in place.

Color the wooden parts with Trans Tint dye. Mix the dye with alcohol to the intensity you desire. Then add several top coats for a certain level of sheen and protection. I used a spray lacquer from a can.

SEVEN Lacing the corners of the shade is a lot like lacing up a pair of shoes. I prefer to have the cord cross on the underside of the shade. Start with the two ends of the cord coming up through the lowest two holes at one corner. Take each end across the gap and push it down the opposite hole. Crisscross the cords and push the ends up through the next pair of holes. Continue in this manner until the entire corner is laced. Tie the cord off about every five holes or so to keep the lacing tight.

EIGHT The four arms end in a compound bevel that matches the tilt of the shade, Rather than trying to measure and lay out these an-gles, it is a lot easier to plop the shade in place and sketch the angles, essentially scribing the arms to the shade.

TIP Whenever you are coloring wood whether with a dye or a stain, prepare a sample of the same species, sanded to the same degree as what your project is made from. Then test the colors you want to use on the sample before com-mitting to your good stock.

ASSEMBLY

1. Screw the top to the arms with #8 x 1½" wood screws.
2. Thread a hex nut onto the nipple and push the nipple up through the hole in the center of the top. Lock the nipple in place with a second hex nut. Thread the bottom part of a light socket onto the nipple.
3. Push the end of the lamp cord up through the hole in the bottom of the upright. Also push it through the nipple.
4. Screw the top to the upright with #8 x 2½" wood screws.
5. Split the cord into two separate leads and knot them together to keep the cord from pulling back out. Strip the insulation from each lead and fasten the leads to the terminals on the socket. For more details on making the electric connections, see the Introductory Chapter. If you are not comfortable doing the electric work, consult with a licensed professional.
6. Rout the cord through the channel you cut in the base. Glue a square of felt to the underside of the base as a finishing touch.

THE DESIGN FOR THIS ACCENT LAMP DRAWS ON BOTH THE ARTS AND CRAFTS ERA AS WELL AS TRADITIONAL JAPANESE ARCHITECTURE. **WHITE OAK, MICA**

(12) **PAGODA** LAMP

YOU WON'T HAVE TO THUMB THROUGH THIS BOOK TOO MANY TIMES before you realize that my design sense and influences are pretty eclectic. I draw on a wide variety of sources and enjoy mixing things up a bit. In keeping with popular culture, I think this is referred to as a mash up. Today's young people are quite good at it, and sometimes like to think they invented the process. But as I think about it, people who design and make things have been doing this for years ... taking details and ideas from one source and combining them with details and ideas from another.

Consider this lamp for example. In some ways it is a fairly traditional design. It certainly recalls the Arts & Crafts style that was popular in this country about 100 years ago. In particular, I drew influence from the Greene Brothers, architects who worked in and around Pasadena, California designing and building some splendid examples of Arts & Crafts style houses and furniture. But when you start looking into their training and design influences, you find that they, in turn, drew on other cultures for inspiration — notably traditional Japanese architecture. So, in effect, they were "mashing up" things when they built such masterpieces as the Gamble House.

With all that being said, this little accent lamp will add a nice warm glow to almost any room regardless of the style of the rest of furnishings. I chose to make mine in white oak with amber mica to play up on the Arts & Crafts connection, but I think it would look stunning in a dark walnut with silver mica panels or even in curly maple with frosted glass in place of the mica. As you think about building this lamp, consider taking a few risks and doing a little mashing of your own.

Construction is pretty simple, though you'll need to make some precise cuts. The top is mitered together while the four frames that make up the front, back, and sides are assembled with lap joints.

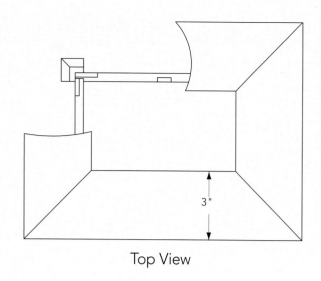

Top View

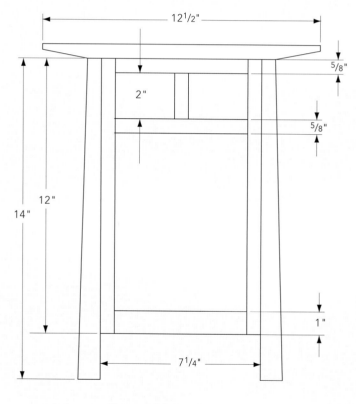

Front View

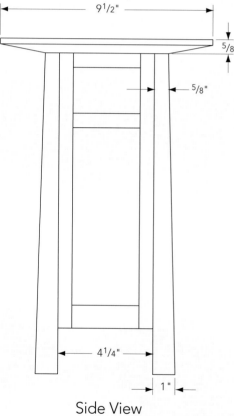

Side View

HARDWARE

#6 x 1 1/4" Wood Screws (4)
1/8 IP x 1 1/4" Nipple
1/8 IP Hex Nuts (2)
Lamp Socket (no switch necessary)
Lamp Cord w/Line Switch

Mica (2 pieces) 7 1/4" x 11 5/8"
(Asheville-Schoonmaker Mica Co.)

Mica (2 pieces 4 1/2" X 11 5/8"

INCHES (MILLIMETERS)

REFERENCE	QUANTITY	PART	STOCK	THICKNESS	(mm)	WIDTH	(mm)	LENGTH	(mm)
A	2	frame front/back	white oak	5/8	(16)	3	(76)	12 1/2	(318)
B	2	frame sides	white oak	5/8	(16)	3	(76)	9 1/2	(242)
C	4	legs	white oak	1	(25)	1	(25)	14	(356)
D	4	front/back stiles	white oak	3/8	(10)	1	(25)	12	(305)
E	4	side stiles	white oak	3/8	(10)	3/4	(19)	12	(305)
F	2	front/back bottom rails	white oak	3/8	(10)	1	(25)	8	(203)
G	4	front/back upper rails	white oak	3/8	(10)	5/8	(16)	8	(203)
H	2	side bottom rails	white oak	3/8	(10)	1	(25)	4 1/2	(115)
I	4	side upper rails	white oak	3/8	(10)	5/8	(16)	4 1/2	(115)
J	2	center stiles	white oak	3/8	(10)	5/8	(16)	3 1/4	(82)
K	4	fillers	white oak	3/8	(10)	3/8	(10)	2	(51)
L	1	bottom	birch ply	1/4	(6)	4 1/2	(115)	7 1/4	(184)

Fabrication

Cut the pieces for the frame to the thickness and width stated in the Materials List but leave them long for now.

Set your miter gauge to 45° and cut the pieces to length, mitering them in the process. Use a stop to control the lengths of the pieces as shown in Photo 1.

ONE Miter one end of each piece first, then use an angled stop block to control the length of the pieces when you make the second cuts. The angled stop block works better than a regular stop as it offers a broader surface in contact with the workpiece.

Glue the frame together. Gluing mitered frames is a tricky business at best. I find using two pairs of clamps allows me to fine tune the clamping pressure as shown in Photo 2.

While the frame is drying, cut the legs to the size specified in the Materials List.

Chuck a ⅜" rabbeting bit in your table-mounted router and cut a ⅜" × ⅜" rabbet along the length of each leg as shown in Photo 3.

TIP When cutting boards into thin strips, the thin strips often warp slightly. To combat this, cut the piece oversize to begin with. Then joint away any warp and cut them to final size.

TWO As you glue the frame pieces together, you can tweak the fit of the joints by varying the clamp pressure. Put a piece of scrap plywood on top of the bottom set of clamps to help balance the pieces as you get things in position.

THREE Rabbet the legs on the router table. Make several light passes, rather than one heavy one.

Taper the two adjacent, non-rab-beted sides of each leg. Each leg should taper from 1" square at the bottom to ⅝" square at the top. Make these cuts on the table saw, pushing the pieces through the cuts on a carrier board as shown in Photo 4. To set up the carrier board, lay out the taper on one side of the leg. Hold the leg on the carrier board with the layout line running right along the carrier board's edge. Screw a fence and a stop block to the carrier board to hold the leg in this position. Adjust the saw's fence to cut right along the edge of the carrier board. Cut each leg twice. Make the first cut with the leg loaded into the jig with the rab-beted corner up and towards the fence. Make the second cut with the rabbeted corner down and toward the fence.

Once the glue dries, cut slots in the frame corners for splines to reinforce the joints. Set the table saw's blade height to 1½" and hold the frame in a cradle jig as you make the cuts as shown in Photo 5. There are plans for the cradle jig shown on page 73.

FOUR When tapering narrow pieces such as the legs for this lamp, I'll attach a toggle clamp to the tapering jig to hold the workpiece rather than getting my fingers too close to the blade. Make sure the clamp is clear of the blade, and check to make sure it's pressure keeps the workpiece loaded squarely and securely.

FIVE When cutting the spline grooves, hold the frame in the cradle jig with its top surface against the jig's face. Locate the slots ⅛" in from the top surface. I find using a clamp to hold the piece in the jig gives me a much cleaner cut than trying to hold it by hand.

Tilt the blade on your saw over to a 79° angle and bevel the underside of the frame as shown in Photo 6. The profile you are trying to create is shown in the Top Frame Section Detail.

Cut the rails and stiles to the dimensions given in the Materials List. Make a few extra pieces you can use to test the joinery setups and to use in case of a mistake (not that you'll be making any, of course!).

The stiles and rails that make up the front, back, and side frames are joined with lap joints. On all four of the

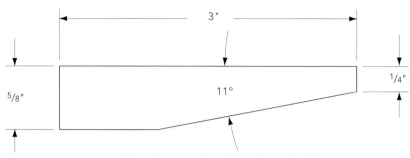

3"

5/8"   11°   1/4"

Top Frame Section Detail

6

SIX Run the frame on edge with the blade tilted to bevel its underside. If your saw tilts to the left, you can make the cuts with the fence to the right of the blade. If your saw tilts to the right, you'll need to move the fence to the left of the blade. Aim to have the bevel just miss the spline.

frames, the outer stiles lap over the rails. On the front and back frames, the rails then lap over the center stiles. Cut the joints with a dado installed on the table saw. Rather than trying to match the exact width of the dado to the width of the pieces, I make the dado somewhat narrower (9/16") and then make two passes to make the cuts the width I need. Set the height of the dado to half the thickness of your rails and stiles (3/16" +/-).

Make the cuts on the stiles first. All eight stiles get the same three cuts — two 5/8"-wide notches near the top end and a 1"-wide notch at the bottom. The placement of these notches is shown in the Front View. Make the cuts by guiding the stiles past the dado with the miter gauge. Use a stop to keep the location of the cuts consistent from piece to piece. For the top two notches, make one cut, then use shims between the end of the workpiece and stop (Photo 7) to make the cut wider until the mating rail just fits in.

SEVEN Use a stop to insure that notches in the stiles are consistent from piece to piece. To make the cuts slightly wider, insert shims between the stop and the end of the workpiece. I find playing cards make excellent shims.

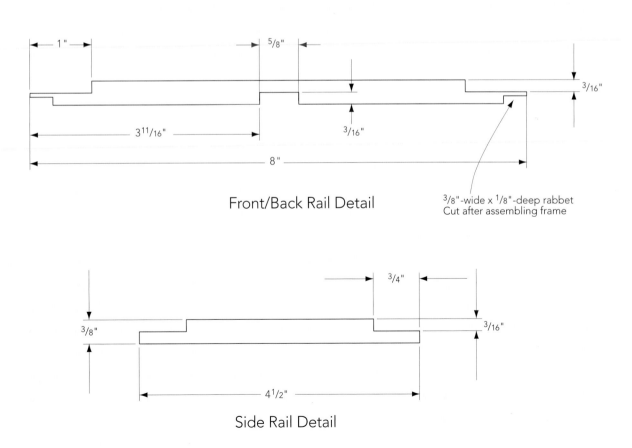

1"   5/8"   3/16"

3 11/16"   3/16"

8"

3/16"

Front/Back Rail Detail

3/8"-wide x 1/8"-deep rabbet
Cut after assembling frame

3/4"

3/8"   3/16"

4 1/2"

Side Rail Detail

For the wider notches at the bottom, you'll want to reset the stop to make the notch wide enough for the wider rails.

Notch the rails in a similar manner to the way you cut the stiles. The dimensions and placement of the rail notches are shown in the Front/Back Rail Detail and in the Side Rail Detail. Note: the drawing shows a ⅜" × ⅛" rabbet in the ends of the front and back rails. Don't worry about this yet. You'll cut it after the frames are assembled. Also notch the ends of the center stiles.

Glue the stiles and rails together to make up the four frames.

Cut ⅜"-wide × ⅛"-deep rabbets along three sides of the front and back frames with a ⅜" rabbeting bit in a table-mounted router (it's probably still in there from rabbeting the legs). Rabbet both sides and the bottom edges of the frames on the inside face.

Glue the four frames together as shown in Photo 8. The edges of the side frames should fit into the rabbets you just cut in the front and back frames.

Clean up any squeeze-out from gluing the four frames together and glue the legs to the four corners of the frame assembly as shown in Photo 9. Cut and glue four filler pieces in the rabbets at the bottom of the legs.

Cut a rectangle of ¼" birch plywood to fit inside the frame assembly — it should fit into the shallow rabbet you cut in the bottom edges of the front and back frames.

Drill a ¹³⁄₃₂"-diameter hole through the center of the plywood. Glue the plywood in place inside the frames.

Cut four pieces of mica to fit against the insides of the lamp. I find mica cuts well on the table saw. Use a fine blade and a zero-clearance throat plate to give the mica plenty of support. Glue the pieces to the insides of the lamp. The folks at Asheville-Schoonmaker Mica Company recommend epoxy for this purpose, but I have also had good results with Hot Stuff CA glue.

Drill four ³⁄₁₆"-diameter holes through the top frame for attaching the frame to the base. Counterbore the holes with a ⅜"-diameter bit to accept the plugs that will hide the screws. Position the holes on the front and back sides of the frame about 1½" from the corners.

Screw the frame to the base, drilling ³⁄₃₂"-diameter pilot holes first, to avoid splitting the thin rail pieces. Plug the holes with ⅜"-diameter plugs and sand them flush.

Finish the lamp with your favorite wood finish. I finished mine with Watco Danish Oil. Try to avoid getting the finish on the inside surfaces of the frames where the mica goes.

EIGHT Glue the four frames together to form a rectangle. Check this assembly carefully for square by measuring across the diagonals. The two measurements should be equal.

NINE Glue the four legs to the outside of the frame assembly. Tighten the clamps gently to avoid miss-positioning the legs.

8

ASSEMBLY

1. Push a ⅛ IP nipple through the hole in the center of the plywood and lock it in place with hex nuts.
2. As with any wiring project, if you aren't comfortable making the connections, consult with a licensed professional. Thread a socket base onto the nipple inside the lamp. Push a length of lamp cord up through the nipple and pull it out the top of the lamp.
3. Split the cord into its two individual conductors and tie an underwriters knot to keep any strain on the wire from pulling against the electrical connections.
4. Strip the insulation from the conductors and attach them to the terminals on the socket interior. The ribbed wire should go to the silver terminal and the non-ribbed wire to the brass terminal.
5. Slip the socket shell and insulator over the socket interior. Pull the lamp cord back into the lamp and snap the socket into place in its base.

WITH IT'S OCTAGONAL WOODEN SHADE AND TAPERED COLUMN, THIS FLOOR LAMP WILL MAKE A HANDSOME ADDITION TO ANY ROOM. **BASE AND COLUMN: ASH, SHADE: CHERRY PLYWOOD**

13 **PENCIL POST** LAMP

THE IDEA FOR THIS LAMP came as I was putting the final touches on the trapezoid lamps. Essentially I was wondering if I could stretch the tapered form to make a floor lamp. I decided I could, but that a four- or five-foot tall truncated pyramid might be a bit clunky if it tapered from roughly 2" square at the top to about 10-12" square at the bottom (necessary for adequate stability). A more slender form seemed to be in order.

This started me thinking about other types of furniture that make use of long tapered pieces. Table legs came immediately to mind, though they tend to taper from heavy at the top to narrow at the floor. Then I remembered seeing an old canopy bed in the Philadelphia Museum of Art. It is simple and plain, but still quite elegant in form. It features tall, tapered posts that transform from square at the bottom to octagonal at the top. A bit of internet research provided a name for this style of bed: Pencil Post. I didn't spend a lot of time researching it, but the style seems to extend back several hundred years to the times prior to central heating when beds were often fitted with curtains to ward against the cold. As the times changed, these four-poster beds lost their curtains in favor of a top canopy, or ruffle. Now, you often see such beds with the posts simply jutting up into the air un-adorned, echoing the style of yesteryear without the fuss of added textiles.

Slightly modified, one of these tapered bed posts seemed perfect for a floor lamp. I decided to make my version relatively thick to compliment some of the more robust furniture available these days. This makes the lamp a little on the heavy side, but this isn't necessarily a bad feature. The added weight makes the lamp that much more stable and less likely to topple over should Calvin and Hobbes stop by for a visit.

While you could purchase a commercial shade for your lamp, (and if you go this route, take the lamp with you for a test fitting) I opted to make a wooden shade for mine. Having the column taper to an octagon seemed a great opportunity to make an octagonal shade. After cutting a few versions from cardboard, I arrived at the shade shown here. The warmth of the cherry veneer plywood combines nicely with the glow from the mica inserts for a very pleasing effect.

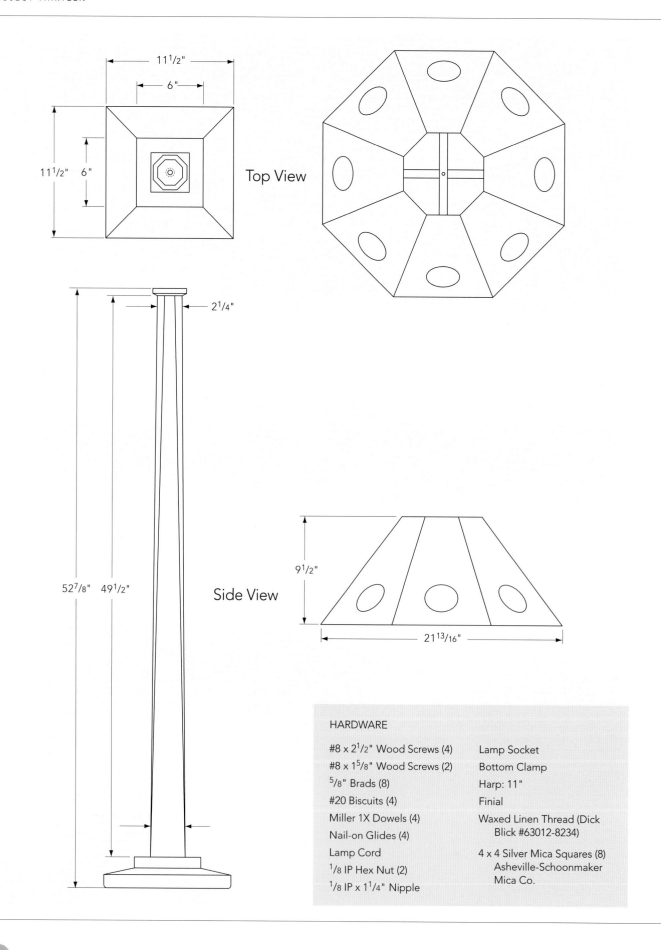

Top View

Side View

11 1/2"

6"

11 1/2" 6"

2 1/4"

52 7/8" 49 1/2"

9 1/2"

21 13/16"

HARDWARE

#8 x 2 1/2" Wood Screws (4)
#8 x 1 5/8" Wood Screws (2)
5/8" Brads (8)
#20 Biscuits (4)
Miller 1X Dowels (4)
Nail-on Glides (4)
Lamp Cord
1/8 IP Hex Nut (2)
1/8 IP x 1 1/4" Nipple

Lamp Socket
Bottom Clamp
Harp: 11"
Finial
Waxed Linen Thread (Dick
    Blick #63012-8234)

4 x 4 Silver Mica Squares (8)
Asheville-Schoonmaker
    Mica Co.

INCHES (MILLIMETERS)

REFERENCE	QUANTITY	PART	STOCK	THICKNESS	(mm)	WIDTH	(mm)	LENGTH	(mm)	COMMENTS
A	2	column halves	ash	1³/₄	(45)	3¹/₂	(89)	49¹/₂	(1258)	
B	4	base pieces	ash	1³/₄	(45)	3¹/₄	(82)	11¹/₂	(285)	
C	1	plinth	ash	1¹/₈	(29)	6	(152)	6	(152)	
D	1	top cap	ash	⁵/₈	(8)	3	(76)	3	(76)	
E	8	shade leaves	cherry ply	¹/₈	(3)	9	(229)	12	(305)	
F	2	shade crossbars	ash	³/₈	(5)	³/₄	(19)	7¹/₂	(191)	

Fabrication

Joint and plane two pieces of 8/4 material to the thickness given for the column halves, but leave them ¼" wider and longer than specified for now.

Set up a ⁵/₈"-wide dado head on your table saw. Set the cutter height to ⁵/₁₆" and cut a groove down the center of each column half as shown in Photo 1.

Glue the two column halves together. After the glue dries, cut the column to its final width and length. As you are cutting the column to width, try to keep the channel centered by removing an equal amount of material from each side. The actual width isn't as important as making the column square. Check the combined thickness of the two pieces and make the width match this measurement.

Tapering the column takes two steps. First you'll taper all four sides, keeping the column square in section. Then you'll taper it a second time, cutting off the four corners and creating the octagon.

For the first operation, choose two opposing faces to cut first. Lay out the tapers for these faces on the adjacent face in between. The taper should go from full thickness at the bottom end of the column to 2¼" at the top end. Set your jointer to take a ¹/₁₆" cut. Hold the guard out of the way and start the cut by lowering the column onto the cutter head so about ¼" of the leading end catches the outfeed table as shown in Photo 2. Push the piece across the jointer. The cut will go from virtually nothing at the beginning to the full ¹/₁₆" at the trailing end. Count how many passes it takes until you are ¹/₁₆" shy of the layout line — it took me eight

ONE Cut matching, ⁵/₈"-wide grooves in the mating faces of the two column halves to create a channel for the lamp cord. The exact size of the channel isn't critical — close is good enough.

passes to get to this point. Repeat the process on the opposing side, making the same number of passes.

Make a second set of layout lines on one of the freshly tapered faces. Taper the two remaining faces in a similar manner, making the same number of passes on each face. To finish up, give each face a final, full-length pass. This will clean up any irregularities from the previous cuts.

For the second part of the tapering operation, tip your jointer's fence over to a 135° angle. Cut the four corners of the column as you did the four faces — lower the piece onto the machine so its leading end drops just onto the outfeed table as shown in Photo 3 and then push it through the cut.

Cut the base piece to the size listed in the Materials List. Cut the ends at 45°, using a stop attached to the fence on your miter gauge (or chopsaw) to ensure each piece is the same length.

TWO To make tapered cuts on the jointer, start the cut by lowering the piece onto the machine so that its leading end lands just onto the outfeed table. Then push the piece through the cut in the normal manner. Make as many passes as need to get the taper you want. Be sure to hold the piece against the fence to keep things square.

THREE Make the corner cuts the same way you made the face cuts except with the jointer's fence tilted. With the depth of cut set to $1/16$", each corner should take six or seven passes.

SHOP TIP To help hold the column as I sanded the various faces, I made up a vee-block from a piece of scrap. This cradled the column and kept it from tipping as I worked. I used double-faced tape to attached some small pieces of cloth to the faces of the block to prevent the block from marring the column.

Preassemble the four base pieces and identify the mating corners with matching letters. Draw matching hash marks across each joint to indicate where the biscuit slots should go. Cut the slots with a biscuit joiner as shown in Photo 4.

Dry clamp the base pieces together. I find that as long as my miter cuts were accurate, I can get all four corners to draw up tight using two pairs of clamps as shown in Photo 5. When you are happy with the way things fit, apply glue and clamp the base together to stay.

FOUR Cut the biscuit slots with the workpiece clamped securely in place. Align the joiner's center mark with the hash mark you made earlier.

FIVE By tweaking the clamp pressure I find I can fine tune the way the four miters fit together. The end nips come in handy for removing stubborn biscuits from their slots after dry clamping.

After the glue dries, scrape away any squeeze out from the base's bottom surface. Tilt the blade on your table saw over to a 75° angle and bevel all four sides of the base as shown in Photo 6.

Round over the four lower edges of the base with a ⅜" roundover bit in a table-mounted router.

Cut the plinth to the size indicated in the Materials List. Cut a ⅛"-deep × ⅝"-wide rabbet across the ends of the plinth's bottom face and ⅛"-deep × ⅞"-wide rabbets along the long grain sides. Chamfer all four edges of the top face. Finally, drill a ¾"-diameter hole through the plinth's center.

Apply double-faced tape to the bottom of the column. Center it on top of the plinth and stick the two pieces together.

Turn the assembly upside down and hold it steady in a vise. Drill four holes through the plinth into the column with a Miller 1X stepped drill bit. The Miller doweling system uses proprietary, stepped dowels to make stronger dowel joints. If you don't have this set up, you can substitute regular dowels instead. Apply glue to the dowels and drive them into the holes as shown in Photo 7.

Center the base on the plinth and screw it in place with four # 8 × 2½" wood screws as shown in the Base Detail, at far right.

Cut the top cap to size and cut its corners off to make it into an octagon. Drill a ¹³⁄₃₂" hole through its center. Drill

SIX Make the bevel cuts by holding the base on edge and tilting the blade on your table saw. Position the fence so the cuts leave a 1⅛" flat on each side.

SEVEN These specialized dowels make a strong joint that is easy to assemble. Because they are stepped, you can insert them most of the way into their holes with you fingers before driving them home with a mallet.

a ¾"-diameter counterbore, ¼" deep from the under-side. Chamfer the lower edges.

Drill and countersink two ⁵⁄₃₂"-diameter holes through the cap as shown in the Cap Detail. Center the cap on top of the column and screw it in place temporarily.

Cut the leaves for the shade to the shape shown in the Panel Leaf Detail on the following page. I cut a 12"-wide length of plywood and then used the miter gauge to make the angled cuts, flipping the piece over for every other cut.

Drill a 3"-diameter hole through each leaf. Drill a series of ³⁄₃₂"-diameter holes along both edges of each leaf as shown. Sand the leaves. When you sand the edges, break them significantly — almost giving them a bullnose profile.

Cut eight 4" × 4" squares of silver mica. (For more details of working with mica, see page 125. Center on the inside of each leaf, covering the big hole. Use cyanoacrylate glue such as Hot Stuff to fix the squares in place.

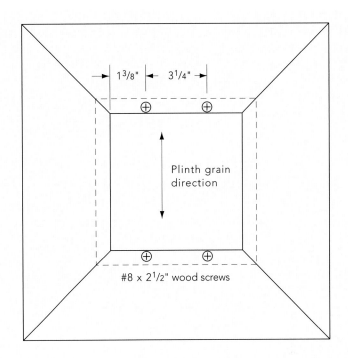

Plinth grain direction

#8 x 2½" wood screws

Base Detail

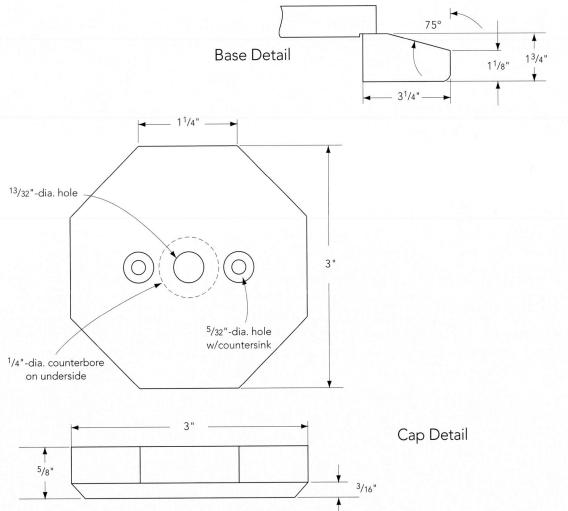

Cut the shade crossbars to the size specified. Set up a ¾"-wide dado on your table saw and cut ¾"-wide × ³⁄₁₆"-deep notches in the center of each piece as shown in the Crossbar Detail to create a lap joint. Glue the two pieces together, leaving the ends square for now.

Drill a ¼"-diameter hole through the center of the crossbars.

Finish the all the wooden parts with several coats of your favorite wood finish. As with many of the other projects featured in this book, the lamp in the photo is finished with Minwax Antique Oil Finish, a wiping varnish.

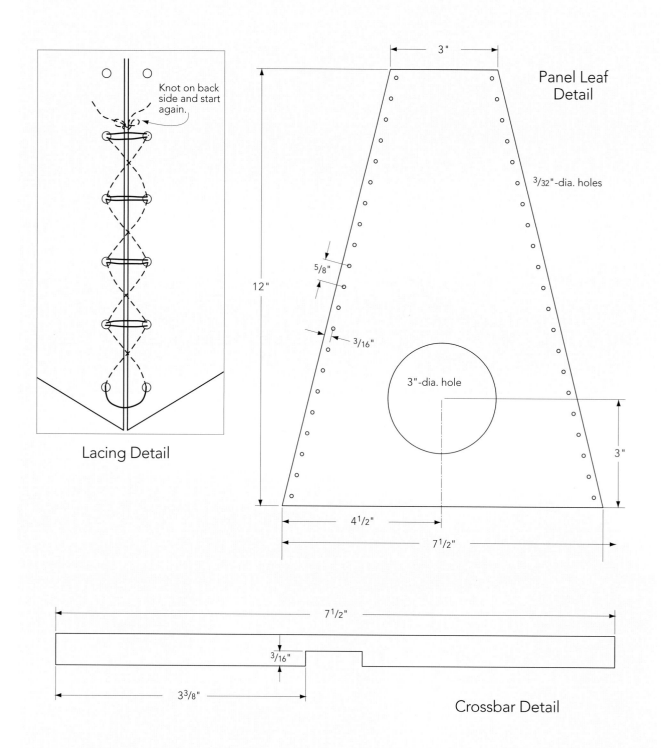

Knot on back side and start again.

Lacing Detail

Panel Leaf Detail

³⁄₃₂"-dia. holes

5/8"

12"

3/16"

3"-dia. hole

3"

4¹⁄₂"

7¹⁄₂"

7¹⁄₂"

3/16"

3³⁄₈"

Crossbar Detail

ASSEMBLY

1. Thread a hex nut on one end of the nipple. Push the nipple up through the hole in the top cap. Slide the bottom clamp on the exposed end of the nipple and lock it in place with a second hex nut.

2. Push the end of the cord up through the hole in the center of the column. Slip it through the hole in the nipple.

3. Screw the top cap to the top of the column.

4. Pop the bottom off the light socket. Slide it onto the end of the cord and thread it onto the end of the nipple.

5. Split the cord into two separate leads and tie them in a knot. Strip ½" of insulation off each lead and attach the leads to the terminals on the socket. The lead with the ribbed insulation goes to the silver screw and the other lead goes to the brass screw. Push the socket into its bottom part. If you are uncomfortable making the electric connections, consult with a professional.

6. Drill pilot holes and hammer in glides at each corner of the base.

7. Lace the corners of the shade together as shown at top right and in the Lacing Detail.

8. Bevel the ends of the crossbars so they fit just inside the top of the shade. Drill pilot holes and attach the shade to the cross bars with ⅝" brads. Set the heads and putty over the holes with Color Putty.

9. Cut the mica sheet into 4" squares. I found it cuts quite well on the table saw. Just be sure to use a zero clearance throat plate to support the mica right where it is in contact with the blade. Glue the pieces to the inside of the shade. The manufacturer recommends epoxy, but I've had good luck with Super-Tee cyanoacrylate (Super Glue). Hold the pieces in place as the glue sets as shown in the photo.

10. Squeeze the harp into the bottom clamp. Put the shade on the harp and fasten it in place with a finial.

Lacing the corners of the shade together is a lot like lacing up a shoe. You can put the cross on either the outside of the inside. My preference is to have it on the inside. Tie the lacing off after every five holes or so to keep it tight.

Center the mica squares over the holes in the shade panels and glue them in place. With Super-T glue, it only takes a minute or so for the adhesive to bond.

THE GRACEFUL CURVES AND INTERPLAY OF LIGHT AND SHADOW IN THE MOULDING PROFILES GIVE THIS FLOOR LAMP
AN AIR OF ELEGANT SOPHISTICATION AND TRADITION. **CHERRY**

14 VICTOR LAMP

THIS DESIGN CAME FROM A LAMP I came across in an antique store. It was an old, cast iron monster with a stained glass shade. Setting up a metal casting foundry seemed like overkill, especially because this book is supposed to be about making wooden lamps. So I took a few snap shots (what did we do before camera phones?) and headed back to my shop to recreate the thing in cherry.

I call this the Victor Lamp because with all the mouldings and shaping going on, it reminds me of a lot of Victorian furniture and even a little of some Victorian architecture. Because it has this classic feel, it will blend in with more traditional décor. As I mentioned, the original lamp had a stained glass shade. Something like that might look good perched atop the stately wooden pedestal. If you opt to go with a purchased shade, take the lamp with you when you go shopping. As my local lamp shade dealer tells me: "Shopping for a lamp shade without the lamp is like shopping for a hat without your head."

As for construction, building this lamp is not particularly difficult, but it is rather fussy. There are twenty-eight small pieces of moulding that need to be mitered on both ends. There are also four larger pieces of moulding that require a cove cut on the table saw and then mitering as you would with crown moulding. By the time you're done (and it will take some time — it took me the better part of a weekend to make all the moulding and cut all the joints) you'll either be an expert at cutting and fitting miter joints, or sick of the whole process; maybe both.

Along with my Accumiter miter gauge, the one tool that made building this lamp go as well as it did is a pneumatic pinner. A pinner is a small nail gun that shoots thin (23 gauge), headless wire nails. This tool made attaching all twenty-eight of those little pieces of moulding surprisingly easy. I actually went out and purchased mine especially for building this lamp.

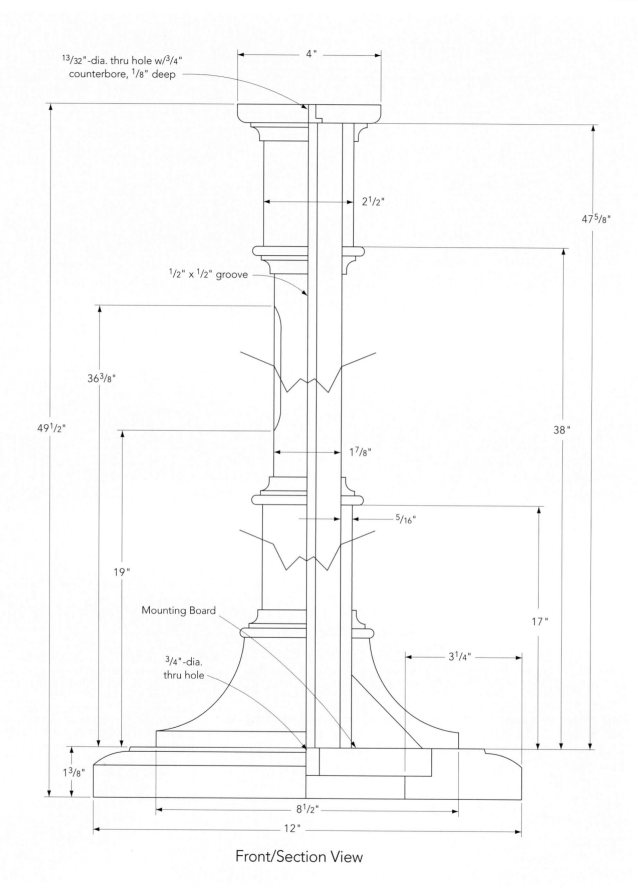

$^{13}/_{32}$"-dia. thru hole w/$^3/_4$"
counterbore, $^1/_8$" deep

4"

2$^1/_2$"

47$^5/_8$"

$^1/_2$" x $^1/_2$" groove

36$^3/_8$"

49$^1/_2$"

38"

1$^7/_8$"

$^5/_{16}$"

19"

Mounting Board

17"

$^3/_4$"-dia.
thru hole

3$^1/_4$"

1$^3/_8$"

8$^1/_2$"

12"

Front/Section View

INCHES (MILLIMETERS)

REFERENCE	QUANTITY	PART	STOCK	THICKNESS	(mm)	WIDTH	(mm)	LENGTH	(mm)
A	2	column halves	cherry	15/16	(24)	1 7/8	(47)	47 5/8	(1210)
B	2	top narrow faces	cherry	5/16	(8)	1 7/8	(47)	9 5/8	(245)
C	2	bott. narrow faces	cherry	5/16	(8)	1 7/8	(47)	17	(432)
D	2	top wide faces	cherry	5/16	(8)	2 1/2	(64)	9 5/8	(245)
E	2	bott. wide faces	cherry	5/16	(8)	2 1/2	(64)	17	(432)
F	4	base pieces	cherry	1 3/8	(35)	3 1/4	(82)	12	(305)
G	1	mounting board	cherry	3/4	(19)	3 1/2	(89)	7	(178)
H	1	cove moulding	cherry	7/8	(22)	4 1/4	(108)	55	(1397)
I	1	cap	cherry	1/2	(13)	4	(102)	4	(102)
J	3	bead moulding	cherry	1/4	(6)	5/8	(16)	21	(533)
K	4	cove moulding	cherry	1/2	(6)	3/8	(10)	21	(533)

HARDWARE

#8 x 1/14" Wood Screws (4)
#6 x 1 1/2" Pocket Hole Screws (6)
#8 x 2" Wood Screws (2)
23 gauge x 1" headless pins
  (several clips)
Feet (4) (Woodcraft #50S41)
1/8 IP x 1 1/2" Nipple
1/8 IP Hex Nuts (2)
Bottom Clamp
Harp
Lamp Cord
Light Socket w/ Switch

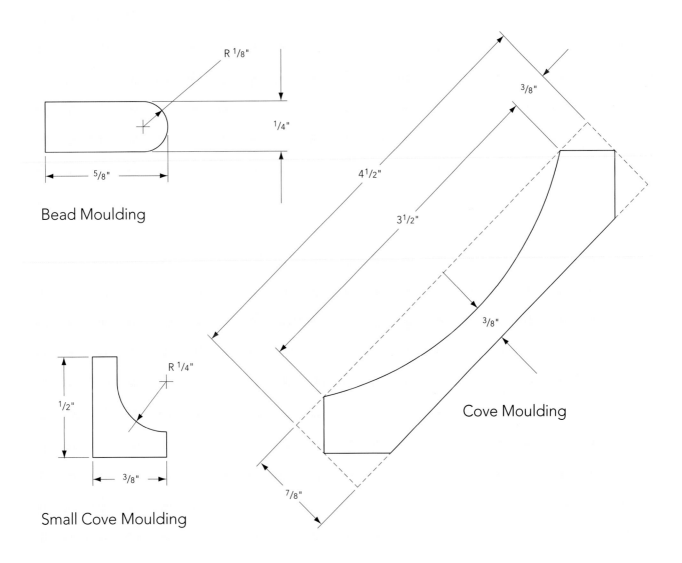

Bead Moulding

Small Cove Moulding

Cove Moulding

Fabrication

Joint and plane the pieces for the column halves from 5/4 stock. Leave them ¼" wider and longer and ¹⁄₁₆" thicker than is specified in the Materials List. You'll have a chance to trim them down later.

Set up a ½"-wide dado head on the table saw and adjust its height to ¼". Cut matching grooves on the inside faces of the column halves as shown in Photo 1. The grooves should be centered from side-to-side and run the length of the halves.

Glue the two halves together with their grooves forming a channel down the center of the of the resulting column for the wires.

After the glue dries, scrape away any squeeze-out. Joint one side to make the pieces flush with each other. Cut the column to its final width on the table saw. If necessary, cut some off of each side to keep the channel centered. Repeat the process to cut the column to the right thickness. Note: it is more important to keep the column square in section than it is to make it to the exact size specified.

Trim the ends to make them flat and square to the sides. Pick one end and call it the bottom. Measure up from the bottom end along the length of the column and make marks at 17", 19", 36⅜" and 38" Use a square to help draw a line around all four sides of the column at each of these locations.

Chuck a 45° chamfering bit in your table-mounted router. Cut ³⁄₁₆" chamfers on all four corners of the column as shown in Photo 2. Each of the chamfers should start at the 19" line and end at the 36⅜" line.

Cut the stock for all the upper and lower faces to the thickness and length specified in the Materials List, but leave the pieces about ⅛" too wide for now.

Glue the narrow pairs to two opposing sides of the column, aligning one end of each with the lines at 17" (bottom faces) and 38" (top faces). When the glue dries, trim the edges flush to the column with a hand plane. Glue the wide pairs in place and trim them flush after the glue dries.

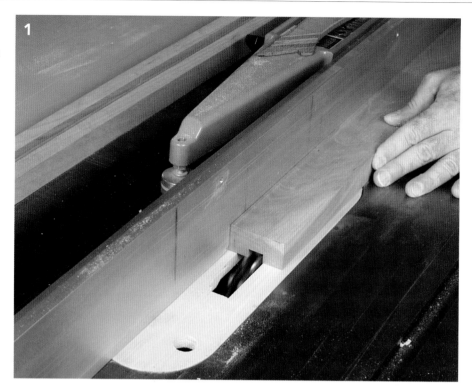

ONE Rather than trying to bore a hole down the length of the column, it is far easier to cut a groove down the length of each halve and then to glue the pieces together

TWO To make starting and stopping the chamfers easier, draw lines on your router table fence that correspond with the outer lines (those at 17" and 38") then use those lines as a guide as you make each of the four cuts.

Cut the base pieces to the size given in the Materials List. Miter their ends at 45° using a stop block to ensure they are all the same length. Cut biscuit slots in the mitered faces as shown in Photo 3.

Glue the four base pieces together. If your miter cuts are true, you can glue all four joints at once with two opposing pairs of clamps as shown in Photo 4. Tweak the tightness of the clamps to coax the pieces into alignment.

Cut the mounting board to the size indicated in the Materials List and drill a ¾"-diameter hole through its center. Chuck a 1" straight bit in your table-mounted router and cut rabbets on the inside edges of two opposing sides of the base. Make the rabbets ¾" deep (cut them in several passes) and wide enough for the mounting board to drop into place. Center the mounting board in the frame then glue and screw it in place with four 1¼" wood screws.

Chuck a table-edge bit in your table-mounted router. Cut a decorative profile around all four sides of the base frame.

Drill holes for pocket screws in the bottom end of the column as shown in Photo 5. Drill two holes in each of two opposing faces and single holes centered on the two adjacent faces.

THREE Make marks across the joints to indicate the biscuit positions. Cut the slots with a biscuit joiner, using the flat surface of your bench as a reference. Be sure to clamp the pieces down to prevent them from shifting.

FOUR By adjusting the relative tightness of the individual clamps you can quickly bring the base pieces into alignment with one another. Check the opening in the center of the frame to make sure the frame is square.

FIVE The column is attached to the base via six pocket screws. A device such as Kreg's Rocket jig makes drilling the holes for these screws an easy job.

SIX The layout for a cove can start as a sketch. The exact curve isn't important, the blade will take care of that. Just make sure the ends of the curve are $3/8$" in from the edges of the stock and that there is $3/8$" of material left at the mid-point. This makes the curve $3^1/2$" wide and $1/2$" deep.

SEVEN In order to position the fence properly, you'll need to know how much blade is exposed when its height is set to match the depth of the curve you are after. Make marks where the blade emerges from the table at the rear of the saw and where it disappears into the table at the front.

Trim the ends of the column if necessary to make them true. Glue and screw the column to the base. Make sure the column is centered, that its faces are parallel to the sides of the base, and that it is standing perpendicular to the base.

Make the cove moulding by running the stock across the table saw against a fence that is clamped at an angle to the blade. This is a process called cove cutting. If you haven't done it before, it may seem a bit counter-intuitive and even intimidating at first. It is however, quite safe — safer, in my opinion, than ripping. Start by cutting a piece of stock for the mould-ing to the size given in the Materials List. This piece is long enough to give you the four pieces you need plus a couple of extras in case cutting the miters doesn't go exactly as planned.

Sketch the cove you are after on the end of the workpiece as shown in Photo 6.

Adjust the height of the blade to match the depth of the curve. If you are working with $7/8$" material, the blade height should be $1/2$" (which leaves $3/8$" of material at the midpoint). Mark the throat plate where the teeth intersect with the plane of the table at the front and back of the blade as shown in Photo 7.

Make up a parallelogram guide as shown in the drawings Coving Fence and Cove Jig Hole Detail. Adjust the two straightedges so they are $3^1/2$" apart (the width of the curve).

Place the parallelogram guide on your table saw so it straddles the blade as shown in Photo 8. Adjust the position of the guide until the rear straightedge crosses the blade at the rear mark, and the front straightedge crosses the blade at the front mark. Mark the saw table to preserve this angle.

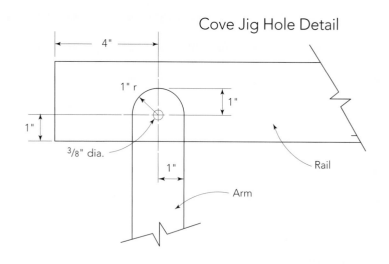

Cove Jig Hole Detail

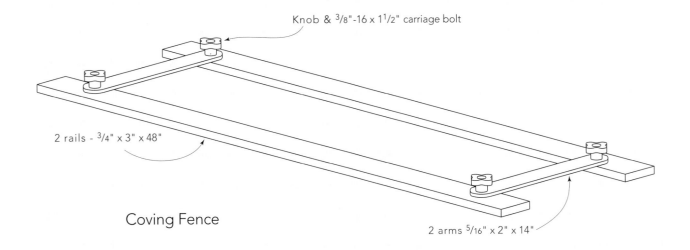

Knob & 3/8"-16 x 1 1/2" carriage bolt

2 rails - 3/4" x 3" x 48"

2 arms 5/16" x 2" x 14"

Coving Fence

Mark a second line on the saw. Make this one parallel to the one you traced from the parallelogram, but 3/8" closer to the front of the saw. Clamp a long, straight board to the saw table along this new line. Often the most challenging part of setting up for a cove cut is figuring out where to position the clamps to they are not in the way and have something solid to grip.

Lower the blade until only about 1/16" is showing above the table. Feed your work across the blade, making a shallow cut as shown in Photo 9. Repeat the process, raising the blade 1/16" - 1/8" at a time until the curve is the proper depth. Keep a pushstick handy to keep your fingers away from the blade.

EIGHT The width of the curve determines the angle of the fence you'll be attaching to the saw. Once you have the parallelogram guide positioned so it intersects with the marks you made, trace along the front straightedge so you have a record of the angle needed.

NINE Cove cuts are made with shallow passes (1/16") to avoid over-stressing the blade. Listen to the sound the cut is making. You'll quickly be able to tell if you are taking too big a bite.

8

9

Tip the blade on your saw to 45° and cut the four corners off of the coved piece to create the profile shown in Photo 10.

Make the miter cuts with a chop saw as shown in Photo 11. Hold the moulding so one of the flats you cut is against the fence and the other is down on the table.

When you are satisfied with the way the joints fit, glue the moulding in place around the base of the column as shown in Photo 12. Use 1" pins to hold the pieces in place as the glue dries. Note: if there are small gaps in the miter joints, force a little glue in the spaces and sand along the moulding to create a glue/dust slurry that will help to disguise the problem.

Cut the cap to the size specified in the Materials List. Drill a $^{13}/_{32}$" hole through its center and counterbore it from the underside with a ¾" Forstner bit. Make the counterbore about ⅛" deep. Round over the lower edges of the cap with a ¼" radius roundover bit in a table-mounted router.

Drill and countersink two $^{3}/_{16}$"-diameter holes, one on either side of the center hole, for the screws that will fasten the cap to the top of the column. Center the cap on the column and screw it in place with 2" wood screws.

Cut stock for the bead and small cove mouldings to the sizes specified in the Materials List. The pieces are long enough to give you some extra in case of a mishap. Note: the pieces for the cove moulding are listed extra

TEN Complete the cove moulding by cutting off the corners. The 45° cuts on the back of the piece create two flats which the moulding will rest on.

ELEVEN Adjust your chop saw to make a 45° cut and make the cut on one end of the moulding. Pivot the saw to cut 45° in the opposite direction and cut the other end. You want the narrow part of the moulding to match the width of the column.

TIP Sanding a cove cut is tedious at best. A gooseneck scraper and a curved sanding block make the task a little less onerous. Sharpen the scraper as you would a regular card scraper. To make the sanding block, trace the curve onto the end of an appropriately-sized chunk of wood. Cut along the line on the band saw. To match the curve on the block to that of the cove, put a sheet of sandpaper in the cove with its rough side up. Scrub the sanding block back and forth to fit it to the curve.

TIP If you don't have access to a pinner, you can use small brads to fasten the moulding in place. Be sure to drill pilot holes. For a perfectly-sized drill bit, clip the head off one of the brads you are using.

TWELVE Spread glue on the flats that rest against the base and against the column. As you add pieces, also put glue on the faces of the miter joints. Pin the pieces in place with fasteners driven into both the column and the base.

THIRTEEN Fasten the bead moulding in place first, then cover it with the cove moulding. You can fill the pin holes later, after you apply a finish.

wide. The idea here is that you can cut the profile along both edges then cut the pieces to width on the table saw. Cut both the cove and bead profiles on a router table. Use a ¼"-radius cove bit for the cove moulding and a ⅛"-radius roundover bit for the bead.

Miter the ends of the pieces and glue them in place around the column as shown in Photo 13. When you get to putting the cove moulding under the cap, make sure you don't glue the cap in place. You'll need to remove it to install the electrical parts.

Screw four feet to the underside of the base. These add stability on uneven floors and create clearance for the cord to escape from underneath. Note, if you order the feet specified in the Hardware List, you'll think they look a lot like wooden wheels. This is purely a coincidence.

Finish the lamp with your favorite wood finish. For cherry, I prefer a natural finish that allows the cherry to darken with age. The lamp in the photos was finished with several coats of Minwax Antique Oil Finish, a wiping varnish that gives a nice luster to the wood.

As a final finishing touch, glue felt to the bottoms of the feet to keep them from marring the floor.

ASSEMBLY

1. Thread a hex nut onto one end of the nipple. Push the nipple up through the hole in the cap so the hex nut lodges in the counterbore.
2. Slip the bottom clamp on the nipple from above and lock it in place with a second hex nut.
3. Thread the base of the light socket on the nipple and lock it in place with the set screw (if there is one).
4. Feed one end of the cord up through the column. Push the end through the nipple and tie a loose knot to keep it from pulling back out.
5. Screw the cap to the top of the column.
6. Untie the loose knot and separate the cord into its two individual leads. Tie these in an underwriters knot. (See the Electrical Section starting on page 8.) Strip the ends of the leads and attach them to the terminals on the socket. The lead with ribbed insulation should go to the silver screw and the other to the brass screw. Pop the socket into its base. If you have an reservations about making the electric connections, consult with a professional.

BETWEEN ITS BROAD SHOULDERS AND COLORFUL, CHECKERED PATTERNING, THIS FLOOR LAMP IS ALL ABOUT PLAYFUL UTILITY. **CHERRY, BIRCH PLYWOOD, COLORED PENCIL**

(15) **DAVID'S** LAMP

AS I HAVE BEEN DESIGNING LAMPS, PARTICULARLY FLOOR LAMPS, I have been struck by how they vaguely look like people. When I began drawing this particular lamp, I started wondering if I could play up on the anthropomorphic nature of its form and make a lamp that resembled someone. The question was: who to use as my muse?

As the design evolved, I drew inspiration from several sources. First is a large painting by Picasso that hangs in the Philadelphia Museum of Art. It features three men, one of whom is dressed in a harlequin outfit. I first saw this painting on a visit to the museum a few years ago and have been back to see it several times since. The harlequin pattern appeals to me, and I've used variations of it on a number of different projects. I also have a colleague at the high school where I teach who is known for his love of brightly-colored sweater vests which often sport a similar, diamond-based pattern and for his trousers with tight, pegged cuffs. As these parts of the puzzle came together, they set the tone (and title) for this lamp.

Construction is relatively straightforward. With all the tapered pieces, however, a lot of the layouts will be traced from one piece to the next rather than relying on the dimensions on the drawings. The part I had the most fun with was the finishing. Instead of turning to my usual stains and dyes, I picked up some colored pencils and used them to create the colored pattern.

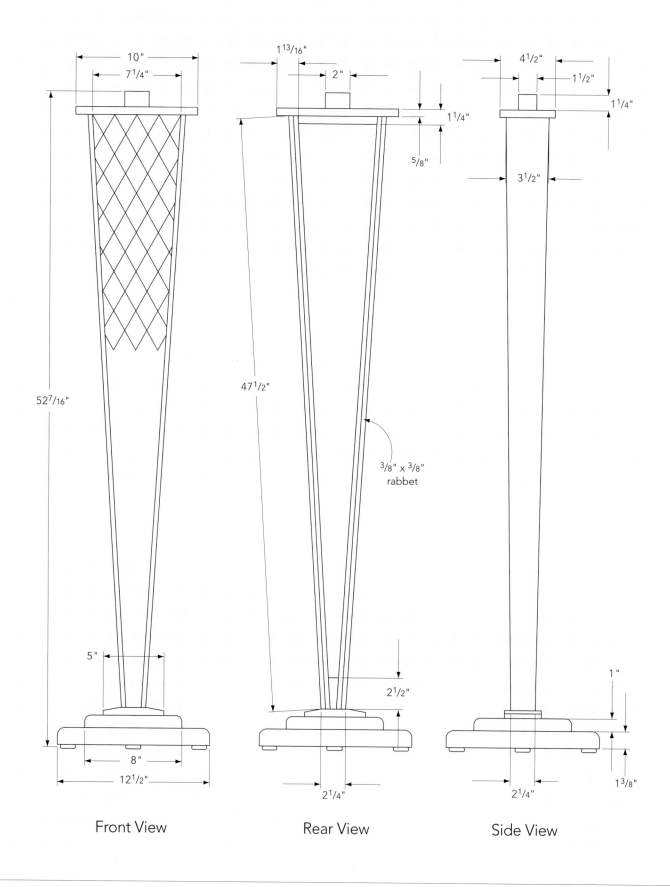

Front View

Rear View

Side View

INCHES (MILLIMETERS)

REFERENCE	QUANTITY	PART	STOCK	THICKNESS	(mm)	WIDTH	(mm)	LENGTH	(mm)
A	1	top	cherry	1¼	(32)	4½	(115)	10	(254)
B	2	sides	cherry	¾	(19)	3½	(89)	47½	(1207)
C	1	bottom	cherry	1½	(38)	1½	(38)	2½	(64)
D	1	plinth	cherry	⅝	(16)	3	(76)	5	(127)
E	1	riser	cherry	1¼	(32)	1½	(38)	2	(51)
F	1	small disk	cherry	1	(25)	8	(203)	diameter	
G	1	big disk	cherry	1⅜	(35)	12½	(318)	diameter	
H	2	front/back	birch ply	¼	(6)	8	(203)	47½	(1207)
I	1	stiffener	cherry	½	(13)	2	(51)	36	(914)

HARDWARE

8 x 1⅝" Wood Screws (10)
#8 x 2" Wood Screws (4)
Feet (4) (Woodcraft #50S41)
⅛ IP x 3½" Nipple
⅛ IP x 2" Nipple
⅛ IP Hex Nuts (4)
Bottom Clamp
Lamp Cord (12')

Fabrication

Cut the top and sides to the sizes given in the Materials List.

Tilt the blade on your table saw to an 86.5° angle and cut both ends of the side pieces at this slight angle as shown in the Front View.

While the blade is tilted, make the shoulder cuts for the rabbets on the top piece as shown in Photo 1.

Return the blade to vertical and make the cheek cuts to complete the rabbets by holding the top on end and running it past the blade as shown in Photo 2.

Layout the taper on one of the side pieces. The piece should taper from 3½" wide at the top to 2¼" at the bottom. Mark the piece so it will be tapered equally on either side of a center line.

ONE The shoulders on the top are slanted in at an 86.5° angle. Locate the top corner of each cut 1¹³⁄₁₆" in from the end and make the cuts ⅝" deep.

TWO Finish the rabbets by holding the top piece on end and running it past the blade. Adjust the blade height so the cuts intersect the angled cuts you made earlier. Clamp a straight edge to the piece that can ride along the top of the fence to help stabilize the piece as you make the cut.

Make a tapering jig by placing the marked side piece on a carrier board. Align one of the tapered layout lines with one edge of the carrier board. Fasten two fences to the carrier board to hold the side piece in position. Guide the carrier board along the table saw's rip fence to make the cut as shown in Photo 3. Make the first cut on the second side using the same jig.

Reposition the fences on the carrier board to taper the second side of both pieces.

Chuck a ⅜" rabbeting bit in your table-mounted router. Cut a ⅜"-wide × ⅜"-deep rabbet in both tapered edges of both side pieces.

Mark a center line on both of the side pieces as well as on the underside of the top. Stand one of the sides in place on the top with the centerlines aligned. Mark both rabbets' locations on the top as shown in Photo 4.

Cut the front and back rabbets on the top in the same manner you cut the rabbets on its ends. Tilt the blade on your saw to match the angle created by the tapered cuts to make the shoulder cuts on the top. Then return the blade to vertical and run the pieces on edge to complete the cuts.

Drill two ³⁄₁₆"-diameter holes near the top end of each of the side pieces as shown in the Side View. Drill a ¼"-deep × ⅜"-diameter counterbore at each hole to receive a plug. Drill ³⁄₃₂"-diameter pilot holes in the top and screw the sides in place temporarily with #8 × 1⅝" wood screws.

THREE To taper the sides, set the rip fence to make a cut right along the edge of your carrier board. Hold the workpiece in place atop the carrier board and make the cut.

FOUR Lay out the rabbets on the front and back of the top by holding one of the side pieces in place and tracing along its shoulders.

Cut a piece of wood for the bottom to the size given in the Materials List. Hold the piece in place between the two side pieces and trace along the sides to mark the taper as shown in Photo 5.

Unclamp the pieces and cut along the traced lines on the band saw to cut the piece to shape. Sand the cut edges to refine the shape of the piece if necessary.

Drill a $^{13}/_{32}$"-diameter hole down through the center of the bottom piece.

Cut the plinth to the size given in the Materials List. Drill a $^{13}/_{32}$"-diameter hole through its center and drill a $^3/_4$"-diameter × $^1/_4$"-deep counterbore from the bottom side. Bevel the ends on the band saw as shown in the Plinth Detail. Also drill and counterbore the four screw holes as shown.

FIVE Catch the bottom in between the rabbets in the side pieces and clamp the piece together. Trace along the sides to mark where the bottom piece needs to be cut to fit in between them.

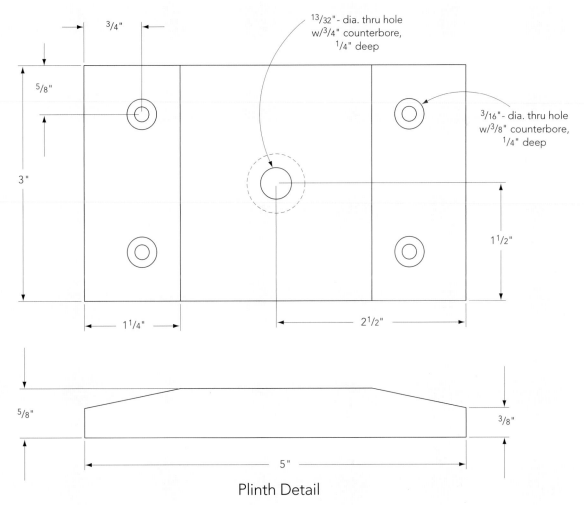

Plinth Detail

$^{13}/_{32}$"- dia. thru hole w/$^3/_4$" counterbore, $^1/_4$" deep

$^3/_{16}$"- dia. thru hole w/$^3/_8$" counterbore, $^1/_4$" deep

$^3/_4$"

$^5/_8$"

3"

$1^1/_4$"

$2^1/_2$"

$1^1/_2$"

$^5/_8$"

$^3/_8$"

5"

Cut the riser to the size given in the Materials List. Drill through the center of both the riser and the top with a $^{13}/_{32}$" drill bit. Counter-bore the underside of the hole in the riser with a $^3/_4$" Forstner bit. Drill and countersink two $^3/_{16}$"-diameter holes in the riser. Screw the riser to the top with two $1^5/_8$" wood screws. Slip a length of nipple through the center holes to help keep the pieces aligned. Unscrew the riser and drill through the top with a 1" Forstner bit. This larger hole will make fishing the wire up through the lamp much easier.

Glue and screw the sides to the top. Use a $^3/_8$" plug cutter to make contrasting plugs for the screw holes. Glue the plugs in place and sand them flush after the glue dries.

Slide a $3^1/_2$" length of $^1/_8$ IP nipple through the holes in the bottom and plinth and use two hex nuts to bolt the pieces together. Glue the bottom between the two side pieces as shown in Photo 6.

Cut stock for the small and big disks to the size indicated in the Materials List. You may need to edge glue narrower pieces to make up a piece wide enough for the big disk. Cut the pieces round with a router equipped with a trammel jig as shown in Photo 7. There are plans for a router trammel on page 30.

Shape the top edge of both disks on the router table. Use a $^5/_8$"-radius roundover bit on the large disk, and a $^1/_2$" roundover bit on the small one. Glue and screw the two disks together with 2" wood screws, making sure their centers are aligned.

SIX Having the plinth bolted to the bottom prior to glue-up allows the plinth to serve as a stop and keep the bottom from squirming out of position when you tighten the clamps.

SEVEN Locate the center of each disk and drill a pivot hole for the trammel. Rout the pieces round with a $^1/_2$" spiral upcut bit or a similar straight bit.

TIP When routing pieces to shape, you may find it advantageous to screw the workpiece to a square of MDF or particle board that is slightly larger than the blank with which you are working. This gives you corners to clamp to that are out of the way of the router as well as a sacrificial surface you can cut into as you complete the cut.

Drill through the center of both disks with a 1½" Forstner bit. Screw four feet to the bottom of the big disk, spacing them equally around the circle. Note: if you order the feet specified in the hardware list, you'll get a set of wooden wheels. These work quite well as feet when the axle hole is countersunk and they are screwed in place.

Screw the upper assembly to the top to the top of the small disk with 1⅝" wood screws, taking care to center it. Fill the screw holes with ⅜" plugs.

Cut the plywood panels for the front and back to the size specified in the Materials List. Lay out a centerline down the length of each piece. Lay out the tapered cuts on each side of the centerline so the piece will fit into the rabbets cut in the side and top pieces.

Lay out the harlequin pattern on the front piece as shown in Photo 8 and in the Harlequin Detail.

Make up a routing jig to cut the angles as shown in the Jig Detail. The jig is pretty simple — just a straightedge screwed at a 30° angle across a piece of plywood to serve as a fence.

Chuck a 60° vee bit in a hand-held router and add a ½" outside diameter guide collar to the base of the router.

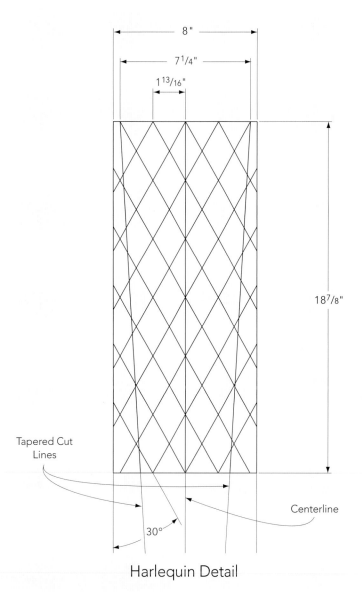

Harlequin Detail

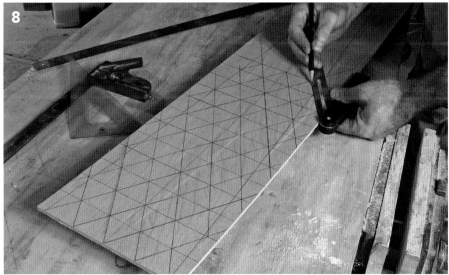

EIGHT The lines that make up the diamond pattern are drawn at a 30° angle to the sides of the piece (as measured before making the angled cuts that allow the piece to fit into the rabbets).

9

NINE Rout all the lines angling one way across the piece, shifting the fence after each line is cut. Near the top, you can cut all the way across the piece. Be sure to stop the cuts where the lines stop towards the bottom.

Position the jig on top of your workpiece with the straightedge against one side and the plywood fence reaching across the piece. The edge of the fence should be ¼" offset from the line you intend to rout as shown in Photo 9. After you rout all the lines angling one way across the piece, you'll have to reposition the straightedge so it angles in the opposite direction to cut the opposing lines.

Cut a piece of stock to serve as a stiffener and glue it to the back of the front panel. Treat the panel gently as you work with it — it will be a little floppy after you complete routing it.

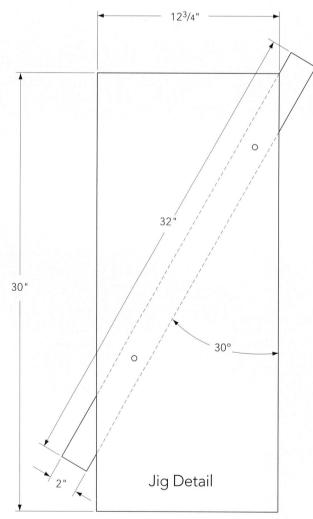

12³/4"

30"

32"

30°

2"

Jig Detail

Use the band saw to cut both the front and back panels along the tapered layout lines you drew earlier. Stay just outside the lines as you make the cuts, then trim the pieces to a precise fit with a block plane as shown in Photo 10.

Spray the front panel with shellac to seal the surface. Then spray the panel with a flat paint to color in the diagonal lines. I used a dark green. Sand the panel to remove the paint from the surface.

Color in the diamonds with colored pencils. I used Prismacolor brand. Then spray over the surface again with shellac as a top coat.

Finish the rest of the lamp (including the riser, which should be detached) with your favorite wood finish. Shellac will work, though I prefer the warmer color that an oil finish provides on cherry. Take care not to get finish in the rabbets.

Glue the panels in the rabbets.

TEN Trim both the front and back panels so they fit snugly in the rabbets in the sides and top. Check the fit frequently to avoid removing to much material.

TIP When routing the ¼"-thick piece of plywood that makes up the front of the lamp, elevate it off the surface of your bench on a similarly-sized piece of ¾"-thick sheet stock. This will provide clearance for the jig's straightedge to hang down below the underside of the panel.

ASSEMBLY

1. Push the end of the lamp cord up through the nipple in the lamp's bottom and feed it up through the hole in the top. Here's where you'll be glad you made that hole fairly large.
2. Thread a hex nut onto one end of a 2" nipple and push the nipple up through the hole in the center of the riser. Put a bottom clamp on the other end of the nipple and lock it in place with a second hex nut. Screw the riser in place.
3. Thread the base of a lamp socket onto the nipple and lock it in place with its set screw.
4. Push the cord through the nipple in the riser, leaving about 3" of cord exposed.
5. Split the cord into two separate leads and tie them together so the cord can't pull out of the socket.
6. Strip about ¾" of insulation off each lead. Attach the ribbed lead to the silver screw and the plain lead to the yellow screw. Push the socket together. See the Electrical Section beginning on page 8 for specifics about wiring. If you have any doubts about doing the electrical work, consult with a licensed professional.
7. Add a harp, shade, and bulb to finish the lamp. As with any lamp, take it along when you go shopping for a shade.

WHILE THE LIGHT CAST BY THIS LAMP IS PRIMARILY DOWNWARD, THE HOLES AND SPACES IN AND BETWEEN THE SLATS DO ALLOW SOME CONTRIBUTION TO THE GENERAL, AMBIENT LIGHTING. **WHITE OAK.**

16 HANGING LAMP WITH SLATS

THE ORIGIN OF THIS DESIGN has its roots in the very early part of my woodworking career. When I was in the Fine Woodworking program at Bucks County Community College there was a class for wood majors that had us visit a lot of places with ties to the industry in and around Philadelphia. One of those places was the Wharton Esherick Museum.

Wharton Esherick was one of the pioneers of today's studio furniture movement. He was an artist who turned to wood as his medium of choice. He made a lot of wonderful, innovative furniture and sculpture in the middle part of the twentieth century. In addition, he designed and built interiors and other architectural details as well as his own home/studio. It is this building that became the Wharton Esherick museum shortly after his death in 1970. If you ever are in the Philadelphia area, it is worth the trip to see it. It sits on a hill overlooking Valley Forge Military Park.

One of the things I remember from that first tour was a lamp Esherick made to hang over his dining table. I've lost the specifics of the design, but I do remember liking the general form and feeling of the piece. That is what I drew on as I developed the lamp you see here. I suspect my version is a little more symmetrical than Esherick's. I'll have to go back sometime to see how my memory of what he did compares to the original.

Essentially the lamp starts out with a wooden hexagon which both holds the light socket as well as serves as a hub for the slats that form the shade. This whole assembly hangs from a pivoting wooden arm which, in turn, is attached to a mounting plate. The cord winds around the arm, allowing you to adjust the height of the lamp by how tightly you wrap it.

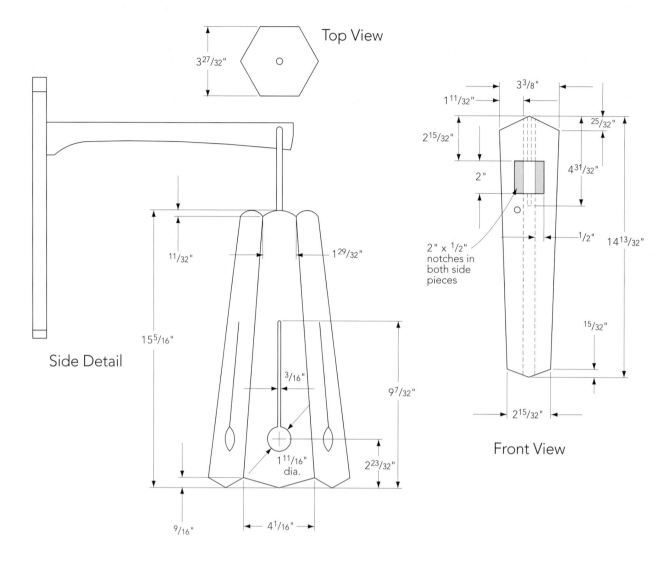

Top View

$3^{27}/_{32}$"

Side Detail

$^{11}/_{32}$"

$1^{29}/_{32}$"

$15^5/_{16}$"

$^3/_{16}$"

$9^7/_{32}$"

$1^{11}/_{16}$"
dia.

$2^{23}/_{32}$"

$9/_{16}$"

$4^1/_{16}$"

Front View

$3^3/_8$"

$1^{11}/_{32}$"

$2^{15}/_{32}$"

$^{25}/_{32}$"

2"

$4^{31}/_{32}$"

$^1/_2$"

$14^{13}/_{32}$"

2" x ½"
notches in
both side
pieces

$^{15}/_{32}$"

$2^{15}/_{32}$"

Fabrication

Mill stock for the arm, mounting plate, and hexagon to the sizes given in the Materials List. Also cut the pieces for the slats. I resawed those for my lamp on the band saw. If you go this route, leave the pieces on the thick side. This way, if they warp after being resawn, you'll have a little material to work with to make them flat again.

Rip the piece for the mounting plate into three strips. Make the outer two 1½" wide which should leave the center piece about ⅞" wide. Joint the sawn edges to prepare the pieces to glue back together.

ONE Drill a ¼" hole down through the center of the short piece of the mounting block. Hold the piece with a handscrew to improve your grip and keep the piece from slipping out of your fingers.

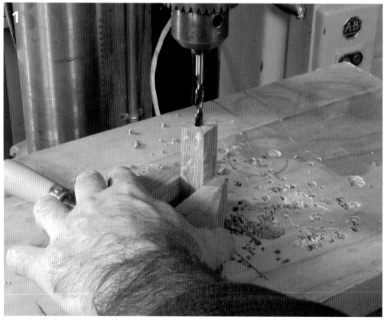

INCHES (MILLIMETERS)

REFERENCE	QUANTITY	PART	STOCK	THICKNESS	(mm)	WIDTH	(mm)	LENGTH	(mm)
A	1	mounting plate	white oak	7/8	(22)	4 1/8	(105)	16	(406)
B	1	arm	white oak	7/8	(22)	2	(51)	16 1/2	(419)
C	1	hexagon blank	white oak	7/8	(22)	4 1/4	(108)	6 1/4	(158)
D	6	slats	white oak	5/16	(8)	4 1/2	(115)	17	(432)

Note: All dimensions are oversized to allow for final sizing.

HARDWARE

1/4" x 5 1/2" Steel rod

#8 x 1 1/4" Super Round Washer Head
   Screws (6) (Mcfeely's # 812-SRZ)

#8 x 2 1/2" Wood Screws (2)

#8 Finish Washers (2)

1/8 IP x 1 1/2" Nipple

1/8 IP hex nuts (2)

Lamp socket with pull chain switch

15' Lamp Cord

TWO Reassemble the four pieces of the mounting plate so you can drill the remainder of the pivot hole into the longer of the middle pieces. While there will eventually be a gap between the two pieces, butt them together for this process.

TIP When resawing lumber, do your cutting several days ahead of when you'll actually need the material. This will give it a chance to adjust to its new state. Store the pieces with stickers in between them and a weight on top to help them stay flat.

Cut a piece 2¾" long off one end of the middle piece and set this short piece aside. Cut the middle piece a second time to make it 11" long. Remove the waste from the same end you cut to make the short piece.

Draw diagonal lines across one end of the short piece to mark its center. Drill a ¼" hole through the length of the piece as shown in Photo 1. This hole will serve as the pivot for the arm.

Clamp the two middle pieces of the mounting plate in between the two outer pieces as shown in Photo 2. Use the hole in the short piece as a guide to continue the hole into the longer piece.

Set up a ¾" wide dado head (the exact width isn't critical) on your table saw. Cut matching notches on the inside edges of the outer pieces of the mounting plate. Start the notches 2¾" in from the top end of the pieces and make them 2" wide and ½" deep as shown in the Front View.

2

Edge glue the four pieces back together to reassemble the mounting plate as shown in Photo 3.

Drill a ¼"-diameter hole at one end of the arm and a ⅜"-diameter hole at the other end as shown in the Arm Detail. Round over both sides of the end with the ¼" hole with a ⅜" roundover bit in a table-mounted router. Cut the arm to shape on the band saw and sand the sawn edges to refine the curves.

Taper the arm on your jointer as shown in Photo 4. Set the depth of cut to 1⁄16" and clamp a stop block to the infeed table so the leading end drops just onto the outfeed table. Three passes on each side should give you the right taper. Make one final, full length pass on each side to smooth out the lumps where the tapers start.

Round over the edges of the arm with a 3⁄16" roundover bit in a table-mounted router. Stop the roundovers where the knuckle begins as shown in the Arm Detail

Cut the mounting plate to the shape shown in the Front View on the band saw. Sand the sawn edges to clean them

THREE As you glue the mounting plate back together, make sure the ends of the middle pieces align with the ends of the notches in the outer pieces.

FOUR To taper on the jointer, start the piece with its leading edge on the outfeed table. Once you've dropped the piece onto the cutter, push it across the machine as usual. You may find it easier to do this with the guard removed as I show here. Just be very cautious of the exposed knives.

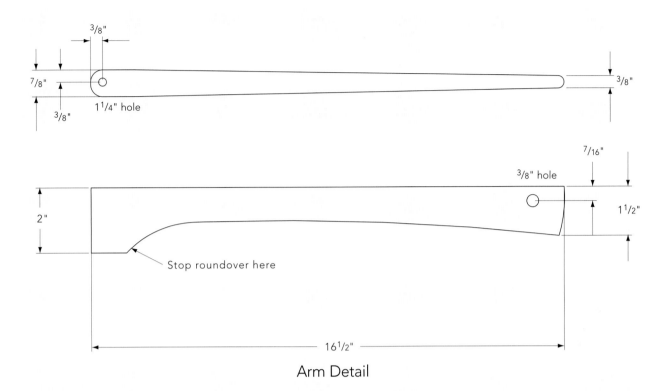

3/8"

7/8"

3/8"

1 1/4" hole

3/8"

7/16"

3/8" hole

1 1/2"

2"

Stop roundover here

16 1/2"

Arm Detail

up. Round over all of the outside edges on the front of the plate with a ³⁄₁₆" roundover bit in a table-mounted router.

Drill a ³⁄₈" hole through the mounting plate as shown. Chuck a ³⁄₈" straight bit in your table-mounted router and cut a ³⁄₈"-deep groove in the back of the mounting plate. This groove should run from the ³⁄₈" hole to the bottom edge of the plate. Also drill the two ³⁄₁₆" mounting holes.

Make up a jig to cut the hexagon as shown in the Hexagon Jig diagram. The jig is quite basic — just a carrier board with a dowel and a removable fence. Drill a ¼" hole through the center of the hexagon blank. Drop the blank onto the dowel and screw it to the carrier board through the forward, right-hand corner with its long edge aligned with the edge of the carrier board. Tilt the blade on your table saw to 83° and make the first cut as shown in Photo 5.

To make the second and subsequent cuts, unscrew the blank from the jig. Rotate the piece clockwise until the freshly cut edge is resting at a 60° angle to the blade. Fasten the removable

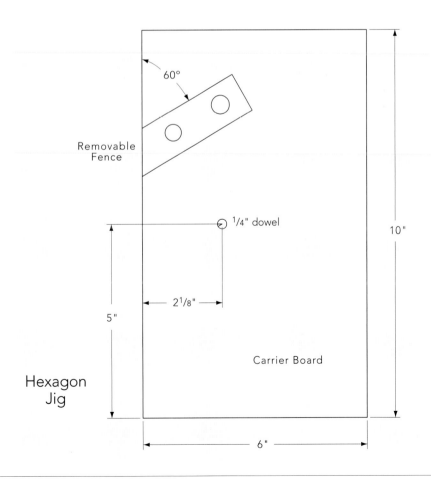

60°

Removable
Fence

¼" dowel

2 1/8"

5"

10"

Carrier Board

6"

**Hexagon
Jig**

FIVE To make the first cut, adjust the table saw's rip fence so the blade cuts right along the upper edge of the blank. Push the jig past the blade, making the cut. The first time you do so, you'll remove a portion of the carrier board along with the waste on the blank.

SIX Once you have established the first cut, use it as a reference for the second cut, and so on. Attach a fence to the jig at a 60° angle to the blade to serve as an indexer.

fence to the carrier board along this edge. Hold the blank against the fence as you make the cut as shown in Photo 6. Cut the remaining sides to complete the hexagon.

Lay out a center line down the length of one of the slats. Mark the center of the 1½" hole along this line. Also mark the upper end of the ³⁄₁₆" slot. The dimensions for these features are shown in the Side View.

Drill the big hole in each slat with a 1½" Forstner bit. Position a fence and a stop on the drill press table so the holes' location stays consistent from slat to slat.

Chuck a ³⁄₁₆" straight bit in your table-mounted router. Use a fence to locate the cut in the center of each slot. Start the cuts in the big hole and use a stop block clamped to the left of the bit to control their length. Make the cuts in several passes to avoid stressing the bit.

Set up a dado on your table saw. Adjust it to make a ¹⁄₁₆"-deep cut and adjust its width to match the thickness of the hexagon. You may have to fiddle with this a little because of the angled cuts on the hexagon. You want to cut dadoes wide enough that the hexagon will slide into and seat with its angled face against the bottom of the dado.

Cut a ¹⁄₁₆"-deep dado across each slat near the top to locate the slat on the hexagon. Guide the pieces past the cutter with the miter gauge and use a stop to make the location of the dadoes consistent from slat to slat.

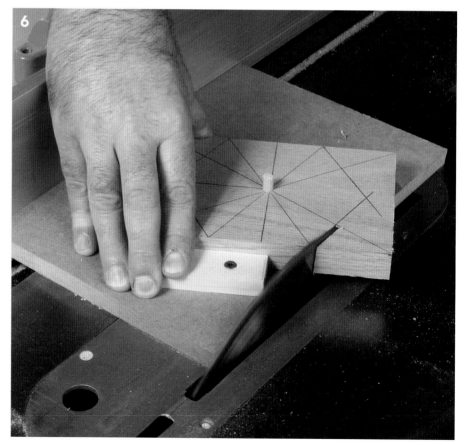

Lay out the tapers on one of the slats as shown in the Side View. Use this slat to set up a tapering jig. This is another simple jig, consisting of a rectangular carrier board with two attached fences. To locate the fences, hold the marked slat on the carrier board with one of the taper lines aligned with the left edge of the board. Screw the two fences to the carrier board to hold the slat in this position. Make the first taper cut on each of the slats as shown in Photo 7.

Make the rounded cuts at the top end of each slat on the band saw and the angled cut at the bottom end using the miter gauge on the table saw. Sand the curves to make them smooth. Roundover all the outside edges of each slat with a ⅛" roundover bit in your table-mounted router.

Drill a ³⁄₁₆" hole through the center of each of the dado cuts for the screws that will attach the slats to the hexagon.

Finish the lamp with your favorite wood finish. I finished the lamp in the photos with several coats of Watco Oil — an oil/varnish blend that dries to a pleasing matte finish.

7

SEVEN Make one taper cut on each of the slats. Then reposition the fences on the jig to make the taper cut on the opposite side.

ASSEMBLY

1. Drill a ¹³⁄₃₂" hole through the center of the hexagon, using the existing hole as a guide.
2. Thread a hex nut onto one end of the 1½" nipple and push the nipple down through the hole in the hexagon. Lock the nipple in place with a second nut.
3. Thread the base of the socket onto the end of the nipple.
4. Put the arm in the notch and pin it in place with a length of ¼" steel rod. You may need to make the holes slightly bigger to get the rod to fit.
5. Push the lamp cord through the ⅜" hole in the mounting plate. Wrap it around the arm and poke the end through the ⅜" hole at the outside end of the arm. How much extra to leave depends on how far down you want the lamp to hang.
6. Push the end of end of the cord through the nipple and into the socket. Split the two conductors and tie them in a knot to keep the cord from pulling back out. Strip the ends of the wires and connect them to the terminals on the socket. Refer to page 8 for more details regarding the electrical connections. If you are comfortable making these connections, consult with a licensed professional. Clip the socket into its base.
7. Drill pilot holes and screw each slat to one side of the hexagon with a #8 x 1¼" Super Round Washer Head Screw.
8. Install the mounting plate by screwing it to the wall with #8 x 2½" wood screws. Dress up the screws with finish washers. Try to get the screws into a stud if at all possible. Otherwise use appropriate hollow wall hangers.

THE ADDITION OF A LITTLE WOOD CAN MAKE EVEN AN INEXPENSIVE FIXTURE LOOK LIKE A CUSTOM CREATION.
AFRICAN MAHOGANY, GLASS

17 SCONCE LAMP

ON SEVERAL OF MY MANY TRIPS to the lighting aisle in my local home center, I kept looking at the shaped glass shades that are available on many of the commercial fixtures and was wishing there was an easy way to bend glass. Then, on one excursion, it struck me that I didn't have to bend glass, all I had to do was buy a commercial fixture and pirate the shade from it. So I came home with a inexpensive (cheap, really cheap) wall sconce with the idea that I was going to incorporate the glass shade into a lamp.

Once I dug the thing out of its box, I began to rethink my idea. The fixture already had many of the features I needed — socket, switch, and a means of readily attaching everything to an electrical box as well as a means of attaching the shade. Instead of pitching all that, why not simply dress up the fixture with some wood? With this in mind, I assembled the fixture and started holding pieces of scrap wood up to it, doing sort of a three-dimensional sketch. After a few band saw cuts, a little work with the belt sander, and the judicious application of double-sided tape, I had a pretty good idea of the look I was after. At this point it was time to cut some real wood.

Turning to my supply of offcuts, I found a couple short lengths of African Mahogany that I thought would look good; their rich red color contrasting nicely with the glow from the frosted glass shade. After I tweaked the proportions from my scrap wood sketch, I built the lamp shown here in an evening, with the finishing taking place over the next few days.

Construction is very simple — the two sides are joined to the top with biscuits with the fixture's base screwed in between. One of my favorite aspects of the design is the apparent complexity of the top piece's front curve. While it looks tricky to cut, in reality, it is very simple to do. What looks to be a compound curve is simply the intersection line between the top surface and the front edge. As both of these surfaces are curved, the resulting intersection line is quite dramatic. The holes add visual interest as well as needed ventilation.

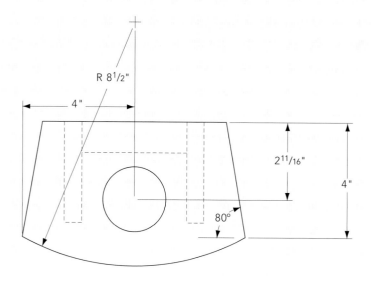

Top View

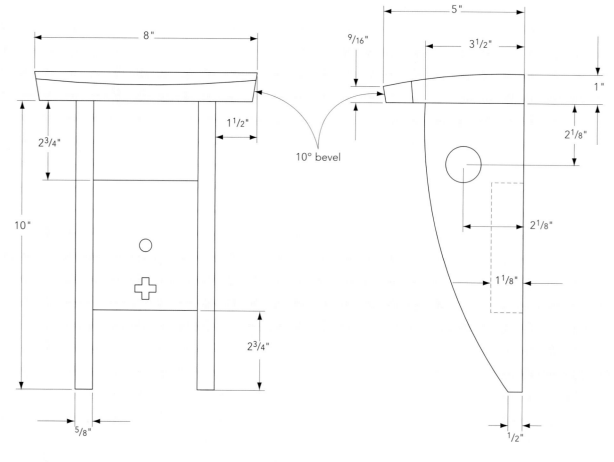

Front View

Side View

REFERENCE	QUANTITY	PART	STOCK	THICKNESS	(mm)	WIDTH	(mm)	LENGTH	(mm)
A	2	sides	mahogany	5/8	(8)	3 1/2	(89)	10	(254)
B	1	top	mahogany	1	(25)	5	(127)	8	(203)

INCHES (MILLIMETERS)

HARDWARE

Hampton Bay Wall Sconce (581-267)
#4 x 1/4" Round Head Wood Screws

Fabrication

Cut the sides to the size given in the Materials List. Lay out the curve on one of the pieces as shown in the Side View. Don't worry about getting an exact radius, just find a thin piece of scrap that you can bend and trace. Cut the side to shape on the band saw then refine the curve on a stationary belt or disc sander. Use the first side as a pattern for the second side.

Lay out the recesses in the sides where they will attach to the sconce's mounting box. These recesses should be 1⅛" wide, ¼" deep and centered from end to end. Cut the recesses with a 1" straight bit chucked in a table-mounted router as shown in Photo 1.

Cut the top to the size given in the Materials List, then temporarily fasten the sides to the mounting box with double-sided tape. You probably will not have to square the corners of the recesses, but you may need to cut a slight chamfer on the sides to accommodate the slight flair around the open side of the mounting box.

With the top piece upside down on your bench, hold the side assembly in place on top of it and mark the sides' location as shown in Photo 2.

ONE Attach stops to your router table's fence to control the length of the recesses for the sconce's mounting box. Use the fence to control the width of the recesses and the bit's height to control the recess's depth. Be sure to make a right and a left hand piece by running one piece with it's bottom end first, and the other with its top end first. Fortunately, because the recesses are centered from end to end, you can use the same stops for both pieces.

TWO Trace the location of the sides on the underside of the top. The side assembly should be flush with the back edge and centered from end to end.

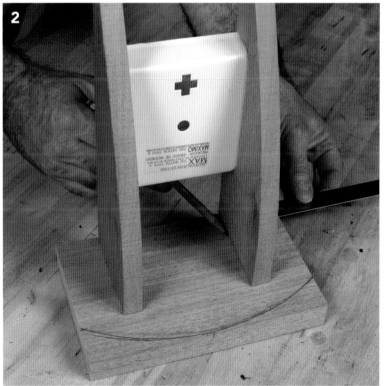

Cut biscuit slots for the joints that will join the sides to the top as shown in Photo 3.

Drill a hole in each side with a 1¼" Forstner bit. Locate the holes as shown in the Side View. Drill a hole through the top with a 2¼" Forstner bit. Locate this hole as shown in the Top View.

Tilt the miter gauge on your saw so it measures 80° to the blade. Bevel both ends of the top as shown in Photo 4.

TIP When drilling through holes with Forstner (and other larger diameter bits) Drill through the piece with a small diameter (³⁄₃₂" +/-) bit first. This will mark the center of your intended hole on both sides of the piece. When you switch to the bigger bit, drill part way through the piece from one side, then flip it and drill from the opposite side to complete the hole.

THREE Clamp one side to the top with the side's top edge aligned with its inside layout mark. Hold the biscuit joiner horizontally to cut the slot in the end of the side and vertically to cut the slot in the underside of the top.

FOUR Bevel both the ends of the top piece. Lay out the cuts so they stop 1¼" in from the front edge. Use a stop block for added support and repeatability as you cut.

Tilt the blade on your saw to 79°. Bevel the front edge of the top as shown in Photo 5. Finish rounding the surface with a hand plane.

Lay out the curve on the front edge of the top. Again, don't worry to much about the exact radius. Grab a thin length of scrap and bend to so it looks right. Trace the curve along the bent piece. You may find it helpful to have some assistance in drawing the line. Cut along the layout line on the band saw.

Tilt the table on your stationary sander down so it creates a 10° bevel. Sand the front edge of the top piece to smooth out the curve and to create the bevel. While you have the table tilted, sand the ends of the top to the same 10° bevel.

Drill holes through the sides of the mounting box and screw it to both side pieces with ¼" round head wood screws. Apply glue to the biscuits and slots. Clamp the sides to the top as shown in Photo 6 with the biscuits in between.

Remove the mounting box and finish the sconce with your favorite finish. The lamp in the photos was finished with a stain and then sprayed with lacquer.

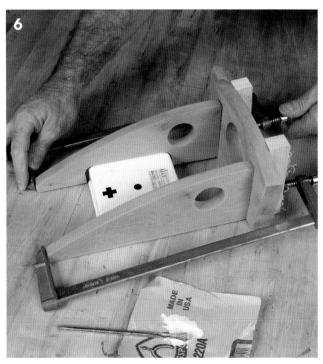

FIVE Hold the top on edge with its front edge down and it's top side away from the fence. Set the fence so the piece will be about 9/16" to 5/8" thick at its thinnest.

SIX To help keep the clamping pressure even, cut some clamping blocks that have a curved face that matches the contour of the top.

ASSEMBLY

1. Screw the mounting box in place between the sides.
2. Be sure the electricity is turned off. Prepare the electrical box as described in the instructions that came with the sconce. The sconce I used requires a cross bar screwed to the box it self with a nipple that threads into the center of the cross bar to attach the mounting plate to.
3. Clip the socket assembly into the cross-shaped hole in the mounting plate.
4. Attach the wires to those in the box — black to black, white to white, and green to bare. Cap each connection with a wire nut.
5. Use a cap nut to fasten the mounting plate/sconce to the wall.

JUST BECAUSE YOU NEED TO REALLY THROW SOME LIGHT INTO A ROOM, DOESN'T MEAN YOU CAN'T DO IT WITH A LITTLE STYLE. **RED OAK WITH WALNUT DETAILS**

18 FLUORESCENT LAMP

THERE IS NO DENYING that four-foot fluorescent fixtures are an economical way to light up a room. But they lack a lot in the way of looks. Even if you purchase an upscale model, they still have a pretty commercial feel to them. So, if you're going to install one (or more), why not take the time to build it a custom enclosure?

This light cover combines the ready warmth of red oak with the dark splendor of black walnut to create an appeal that speaks of the finer things in life. Add to that the exposed joinery and finely executed details and you have a fixture that even Gustav Stickley would lust after.

Construction is similar to that you use to build cabinetry or case furniture — box joints to hold the corners together, miters for the trim, and lap joints for the gridwork. If you've never cut box joints before, you'll need to build a jig to do so. This isn't difficult to do (there are many plans available on the internet for these simple jigs) and once you have it, you can use it over and over again. Cutting the actual joints is remarkably straightforward. Once you're done it a time or three, it will become second nature. I think you'll find it a remarkably useful joint. It is quite strong, relatively fast and easy to execute, and clamps up well.

When you're shopping for your fluorescent unit, it is well worth the extra money to get a commercial grade fixture. While the "Shop Light" units are tempting, I've had really poor luck with them. They seem to work for awhile then fail prematurely. In contrast, I've never had any trouble with any of the commercial-grade units I've installed.

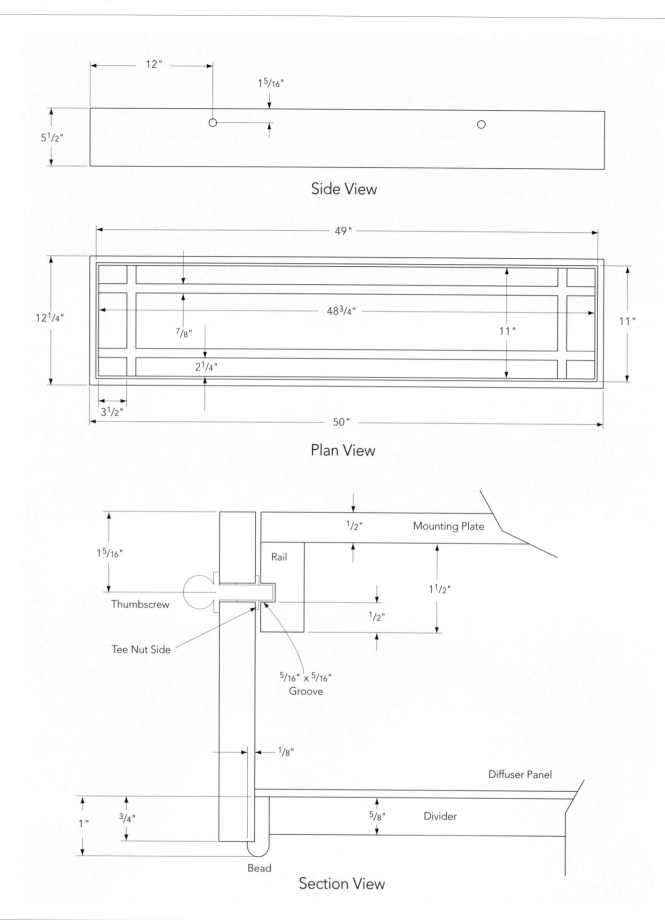

12"

1 5/16"

5 1/2"

Side View

49"

12 1/4"

48 3/4"

11"

11"

7/8"

2 1/4"

3 1/2"

50"

Plan View

1/2"   Mounting Plate

Rail

1 5/16"

1 1/2"

1/2"

Thumbscrew

Tee Nut Side

5/16" x 5/16"
Groove

1/8"

Diffuser Panel

1"   3/4"

5/8"   Divider

Bead

Section View

INCHES (MILLIMETERS)

REFERENCE	QUANTITY	PART	STOCK	THICKNESS	(mm)	WIDTH	(mm)	LENGTH	(mm)	COMMENTS
A	2	sides	red oak	$5/8$	(16)	$5^1/2$	(140)	50	(1270)	
B	2	ends	red oak	$5/8$	(16)	$5^1/2$	(140)	$12^1/4$	(311)	
C	2	long beads	walnut	$3/8$	(10)	1	(25)	49	(1245)	
D	2	short beads	walnut	$3/8$	(10)	1	(25)	11	(254)	
E	2	long dividers	red oak	$5/8$	(16)	$7/8$	(22)	$48^3/4$	(1238)	
F	2	short dividers	red oak	$5/8$	(16)	$7/8$	(22)	11	(279)	
G	1	mounting plate	red oak	$1/2$	(13)	$10^7/8$	(276)	$48^5/8$	(1235)	
H	2	rails	red oak	$3/4$	(16)	$1^1/2$	(22)	$48^5/8$	(1235)	

HARDWARE

10 - #8 x $1^1/2$" Wood Screws

4 - $1/4$-20 x $1^1/4$" Decorative Thumbscrews

4 - $1/4$-20 Tee-Nuts

4 - #8 X $1/2$" Roundhead Sheet Metal Screws

Screws for attaching mounting plate to ceiling

48" Two-Tube Fluorescent Fixture with Tubes

12" x 48" Plastic Diffuser Panel

Fabrication

Cut the sides and ends to the sizes given in the Materials List. Mount a $3/8$" box joint cutter (or a $3/8$" dado) on your table saw. Set up a box joint jig to make $3/8$" box joints as shown in Photo 1. The thickness and position of the pin are critical to the fit of the joint. The first time you use the jig, raise the cutter so it is about $1/2$" above the surface of the jig's base. Make a cut. This will establish a cut in the base and the cut in the fence that will hold the pin. Cut a 2" length of a dense hardwood such as cherry or maple to fit perfectly in the cut. It will be about $3/8$" wide and $1/2$" thick, cut it slightly over-sized. Scrape and sand it to a snug fit. Don't glue it in place — there are times you'll want to remove it. Note: Cut the wood for the pin before you put the box joint cutter on the saw. I frequently forget this and have to tear down the set up so I can cut the pin to size.

Once you have the pin fit, shift the fence over so the pin is one cut's width away from the cutter as shown in the photo. After making a test cut you can shift the position of the pin to adjust the fit. If the joint is too loose, move the pin to the right, away from the cutter. If the joint is too tight, shift the pin to the left, towards the cutter. Often the difference between a good fit and a poor one is just a few thousandths of an inch, so you'll just be moving the pin a little bit at a time.

Set the height of the cutter above the base to be slightly less (<$1/32$") than the thickness of your stock. Make a test joint in scrap to be sure the jig is set correctly. The pieces should fit together with firm hand pressure. To make the joint, start with the first piece against the pin as shown in Photo 2. After

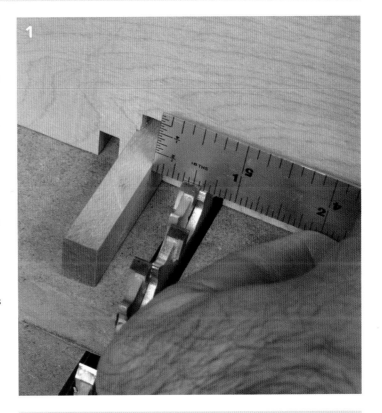

ONE You can get pretty close to the right setting by measurement, but the proof of your set up will be in the joint itself. As you're milling your work pieces, prepare several sacrificial boards the same thickness and width as your good stock to use for test cuts.

TIP If you find your workpieces are tearing out on the back side of the cut as you make box joints, it is probably because the opening in the fence is too big and isn't supporting the wood fibers. In this case, add a piece of ¼" plywood between the workpiece and the fence. This is similar to making a zero clearance throat plate for your table saw. Remove the pin to make the initial cut, creating a slot in the plywood for the pin itself.

making the cut, move the piece to the right so the cut you just made registers on the pin as shown in Photo 3. Start the second piece with a space as shown in Photo 4.

Apply glue to the sides of the interlocking fingers and glue the ends to the sides. Measure the diagonals to make sure the assembly is square. (The two measurements should match.) Because the cutter height was set to slightly less than the thickness of your material, you should be able to use clamp blocks right on top of the joints without the joint itself interfering with squeezing the pieces together.

Set the fence on your table saw to make a ¼"-wide cut. Adjust the blade height to ⅞" and cut a rabbet on each of the bead pieces as shown in Photo 5.

Cut the beads to length so they fit perfectly inside the box frame with their shoulders resting on the frame pieces. Miter the pieces where they meet at the corners.

Cut the long and short dividers to the width and thickness specified in the Materials List. As you cut them to length, check to make sure they fit inside the frame.

TWO Mark one edge of all your work pieces. Always keep this marked edge to the right. For the two end pieces, start the joint with the marked edge against the pin.

THREE Make cuts across the end of the piece, being sure to seat the workpiece firmly down on the base and back against the fence. If the piece isn't seated correctly, the shoulder created won't be the proper depth and the joint won't go together correctly.

FOUR The mating pieces start with a space. Align the marked edge of the workpiece with the right-hand edge of the slot in the base to position the piece. Make the rest of the cuts, registering the cut you just made on the pin.

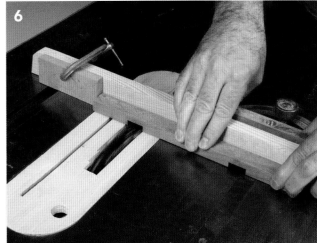

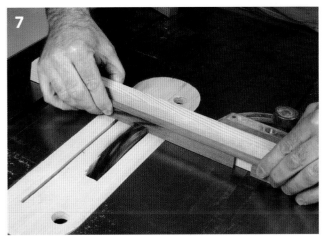

FIVE Rabbeting the bead pieces creates a shoulder that makes the pieces easier to position when attaching them to the main assembly.

SIX Attach a sacrificial fence to your miter gauge that extends several inches on either side of the blade. Clamp a stop block to the fence to help position the cuts.

SEVEN Position the dadoes through the bead pieces using the marks you made when you had the grid in position.

Set up a dado on your table saw. Make the width of the dado match the width of the dividers. Set the height of the dado to be half the thickness of the dividers. Cut dados across the grid pieces to make half lap joints as shown in Photo 6. Place the cuts 3½" in from the ends of the longs pieces, and 2¼" in from the ends of the short pieces as shown in the Plan View. Put a drop of glue in each joint and clamp the grid together. Check the diagonals of the inner rectangle to be sure it is square.

Put the bead pieces in place and temporarily clamp them to the frame with spring clamps. Turn the frame over and rest it on saw horses so you can drop the grid in place. Mark where the dividers rest on the beads.

Raise the height of the dado to match the thickness of the dividers. Cut dados in the bead pieces to hold the grid as shown in Photo 7. Glue the beads in position.

Cut the mounting plate and rails to the sizes given in the Materials List. Cut ⁵⁄₁₆" wide grooves along the length of the rails as shown in Section View. Drill and countersink holes along the edge of the mounting plate then fasten the rails to the plate with #8 × 1½" wood screws.

Drill four holes through the sides of the frame and install tee nuts on the inside surface as shown in the Side View and Section View. These are for the thumbscrews you'll use to hold the frame in place.

Finish the piece with your favorite wood finish. The unit in the photos is finished with several coats of Minwax Antique Oil finish. Note, the grid isn't glued in place. It just sits in the dadoes you cut in the beads. Among other things, this makes it easier to finish.

ASSEMBLY & INSTALLATION

1. Fasten the fluorescent fixture to the mounting plate with four #8 x ½" sheet metal screws. If necessary, drill the plate for the wire first.
2. Fasten the plate to the ceiling. There are so many variables here, it is hard to give specifics. If possible, try to put the mounting screws into solid wood.
3. Wire the fixture according to the manufacturer's instructions.
4. Cut the diffuser panel to fit inside the frame. Plastic cuts well on the table saw. Use a fine tooth blade and be sure to install a zero-clearance throat insert to give the plastic plenty of support. Also make sure your fence is tight to the table so the plastic can't slip underneath it. If necessary, clamp an auxiliary face to the fence to get rid of any gap.
5. Put the grid in place, followed by the diffuser. Hold the unit against the ceiling and tighten the thumbscrews to hold it in place.

EVEN A SIMPLE CIRCULAR CEILING LIGHT CAN BENEFIT FROM A LITTLE WOODEN TRIM WORK. HERE, A COMMERCIAL GLASS DIFFUSER SHADE IS FAMED WITH A SEGMENTED WOOD DISK. **WALNUT**

(19) **CIRCULAR** LAMP

RECENTLY I'VE TAKEN THE TIME to check out the lighting sections in the home centers I frequent, looking for both ideas and interesting products to use in lamps. In every store I've visited, I've come across a selection of glass shades in various shapes and sizes. Many of these are available as replacement parts or as options for use in the fixtures on display.

One of the products I found is called a 12" diffuser — a circular glass dish meant to shade a ceiling-mounted bulb. I brought one home with the thought I could dress it up a little with a wooden frame. One interesting/strange thing about the diffuser I purchased — it is labeled as being a 12" diffuser, but it is actually 13" in diameter. The frame I designed will work for either size, but be sure to measure the diameter of the shade you buy so you know what you are dealing with ahead of time.

Construction of the frame is straightforward, though it does require some precision. There are eight pieces to make, each with two 22.5° miter cuts. This makes for 16 cuts that have to made quite accurately, or the frame won't come together. Fortunately, there is a trick you can use to help compensate for any minor troubles with alignment.

Once you have the frame together, you'll need a trammel for your router to cut it round as well as to cut the rabbet for the shade. There are commercial models available, or you can make one. I've provided drawings for the one I use on page 30.

INCHES (MILLIMETERS)

REFERENCE	QUANTITY	PART	STOCK	THICKNESS	(mm)	WIDTH	(mm)	LENGTH	(mm)
A	8	segments	walnut	$7/8$	(22)	3	(76)	$6^5/8$	(168)
B	4	retainers	walnut	$3/8$	(10)	$5/8$	(16)	2	(51)

HARDWARE

#20 Biscuits (8)
#6 x 1" Brass Wood Screws (4)
12" Diffuser (13" dia.)
Twin Light Socket w/ $1/8$ IP Nipples
$1/8$ IP Decorative Nut
Steel Canopy (or Box Cover)
Wire Nuts

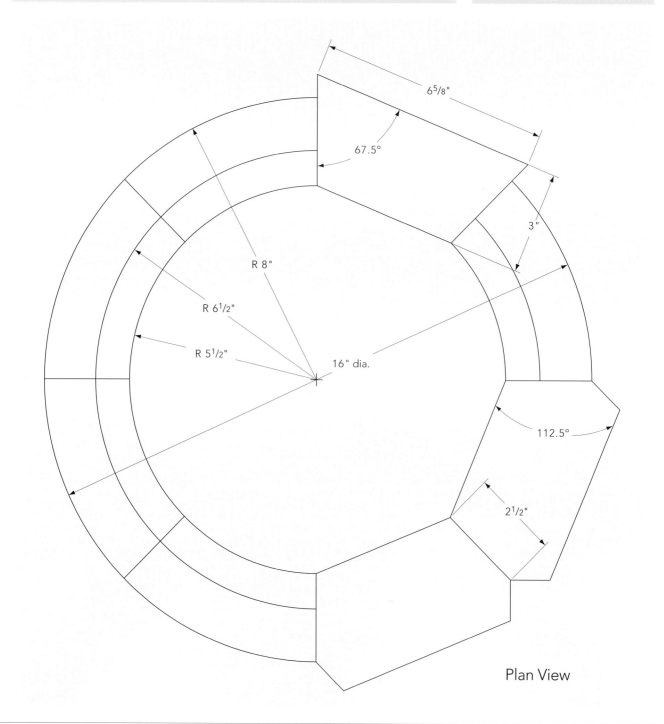

Plan View

Fabrication

Cut the stock for the segments to the thickness and width given in the Materials List. Adjust your miter gauge to make a 22.5° miter (67.5° to the blade) and cut the pieces to length using a stop as shown in Photo 1. It is a good idea to make an extra segment or two to use for test pieces as you make the various setups.

Reset the miter gauge to make a 22.5° miter (112.5° to the blade) and cut off the corners of the pieces as shown in Photo 2 and in the Plan View.

ONE To join the eight segments in a circle, you'll need to be pretty accurate with your miter cuts. Use a stop block to ensure the pieces are a consistent length and to keep them from slipping along a fence as you cut.

TWO As you cut the corners off of the segments, cut one end of each, then reset the stop before cutting the opposite ends.

Cut slots for #20 biscuits in all the miter faces. Center the slots 1" in from the inside corners of the miters. The slots will show on the inside edges of the pieces but this will be hidden when the piece is installed. Be sure to clamp the pieces down as you make the cuts as show in Photo 3.

Glue pairs of the segments together as shown in Photo 4. After the glue dries, glue the pairs together to form two halves.

Check the fit of the miters that will join the two halves. If the pieces don't mate properly, screw each half (in turn) to a piece of sheet stock and run it across the table saw as shown in Photo 5. Lo-

THREE Use the top of your bench as a reference surface for the biscuit joiner. Be sure to cut all the pieces with their better sides facing up.

FOUR As you glue the segment pairs together, place the clamps so they bear on the small flats you created when you cut off the corners. This puts the pressure directly across the joints and help make sure the joints go together tightly.

cate the screws near the outside of the pieces where the holes will be cut away when you make the piece round. Glue the two halves together.

Screw the assembly to a sacrificial surface. Trace around the inside opening as shown in Photo 6. Keep the screws to the outside of the pieces where the holes will be cut away. If you already put holes in the pieces when you screwed the piece to the carrier board to clean up the miters, use those same holes here.

FIVE To trim the mating surfaces of each half to a perfect fit, attach the halves to a piece of flat carrier board with the edges just barely over hanging one edge. Set the fence so the saw will cut right along that edge and run the carrier board across the saw. The cut will trim the two edges in a straight line. After you trim both halves, they should fit together perfectly.

SIX Before cutting the assembly to its final shape, you'll need to locate the center. Start this process by fastening the assembly to a piece of sheet stock that you won't mind cutting into. Trace around the interior opening.

7

Draw lines connecting the corners of the tracing. The intersection of these lines should indicate the center point. Drill a ¼" diameter hole in a piece of material the same thickness as your work piece (I used an extra segment I had made as a test piece). Screw this piece to the sacrificial board as shown in Photo 7.

Chuck a ½" spiral upcut bit in a router. Attach the router to a trammel (there are drawings for one on page 30) and adjust the trammel so the router will cut an 11" diameter circle as measured to

SEVEN If you peer down through the hole you drilled in the extra piece, you should be able to center it accurately over the intersection point of the lines connecting the eight corners. Make sure the screw heads are sunk below the surface of the piece.

the outside of the bit (the side furthest from the trammel's pivot). Rout the inside of the assembly round as shown in Photo 8.

Swap the upcut bit for a 1" straight bit and rout a 1"-wide by ¼"-deep rabbet that fits the diffuser as shown in Photo 9. Pivot the router with the trammel to control the cut.

Drive screws down through the rabbet to keep the assembly in place after you remove the screws near the outside edge. Remove the outer screws so you won't run into them with the router bit as you cut the outside of the assembly.

EIGHT Cut the inside of the segmented assemble round in several passes, pivoting the router in a clockwise direction as you go.

NINE Be sure to have the diffuser on hand when you rout the rabbet it will fit into.

10

TEN Use the fence as a starting pin as you pivot the ring into the cut.

Switch back to the ½" spiral upcut bit and rout the outside of the disk round. Use the trammel to make the resulting ring 16" in diameter.

Shape the outer edge of the ring with a ⅜"-radius roundover bit in a table-mounted router as in Photo 10.

Cut the retainers to the size indicated in the Materials List. Bevel one end of the each to match the contour of the glass diffuser. Screw the retainers to the rings, spacing them equally.

Finish the ring with your favorite wood finish. The unit in the photo was finished with several coats of Watco Danish Oil.

ASSEMBLY

1. This lamp is meant to be installed over a ceiling box with the light socket hard wired to your house's electrical system. If you have any doubts about your ability to attach the wires correctly, consult with a professional electrician. Note, in some communities, any changes to a house's electrical system must be performed by a licensed professional. Check with your local authorities before proceeding.
2. Turn off the power that feeds the ceiling box.
3. Attach the crossbar to the ceiling box. The box should have screws for this purpose.
4. Thread one of the socket's nipples into the hole in the center of the crossbar.
5. Feed the leads from the socket through the hole in the center of the canopy and then through the nipple and into the box. Attach the black wire to the black wire in the box, the white wire to the white wire, and the ground wire (usually green) to the bare wire. Cap all the connections with wire nuts.
6. Screw the canopy to the crossbar to cover the box. Attach the socket to the end of the nipple that comes through the canopy.
7. Place the diffuser in the rabbet and lock it in place with the four retainers.
8. Invert the diffuser/ring and put it in place over the socket with the second nipple extending down through the hole in the center of the glass. Hold the diffuser in place with the decorative nut.

SUPPLIERS

AMAZON
www.amazoncom

ASHEVILLE MICA
900 Jefferson Ave.
Newport News, VA 23607
800-385-7311
www.ashevillemica.com

BUSY BEE TOOLS
130 Great Gulf Dr.
Concord, ON
Canada L4K 5W1
800-461-2879
www.busybeetools.com

**CONSTANTINE'S WOOD
CENTER OF FLORIDA**
1040 E. Oakland Park Blvd.
Fort Lauderdale, FL 33334
800-443-9667
www.constantines.com

DICK BLICK
P.O. Box 1267
Galesburg, IL 61402-1267
800-828-4548
www.dickblick.com

DOVER DESIGNS, LLC
P.O. Box 3644
Hagerstown, MD 21742
301-733-0909
www.doverdesignsllc.com

EAGLE AMERICA
P.O. Box 1099
Chardon, OH 44024
800-872-2511
www.eagleamerica.com

FORREST MANUFACTURING
461 River Road
Clifton, NJ 07014
800-733-7111
www.forrestblades.com

**FRANK PAXTON
LUMBER COMPANY**
5701 W. 66th St.
Chicago, IL 60638
800-323-2203
www.paxtonwood.com

HIGHLAND WOODWORKING
1045 North Highland Ave. NE
Atlanta, GA 30306
800-241-6748
www.highlandwoodworking.com

HORTON BRASSES INC.
49 Nooks Hill Road
Cromwell, CT 06416
800-754-9127
www.horton-brasses.com

JESSEM TOOL COMPANY
124 Big Bay Point Rd.
Barrie, Ontario
L4N 9B4
866-272-7492
www.jessem.com

KLINGSPOR ABRASIVES INC.
2555 Tate Blvd. SE
Hickory, N.C. 28602
800-645-5555
www.klingspor.com

LEE VALLEY TOOLS LTD.
P.O. Box 1780
Ogdensburg, NY 13669-6780
800-871-8158 (U.S.)
800-267-8767 (Canada)
www.leevalley.com

LOWE'S COMPANIES, INC.
P.O. Box 1111
North Wilkesboro, NC 28656
800-445-6937
www.lowes.com

MCFEELY'S
P.O. Box 44976
Madison, WI 53744-4976
800-443-7937
www.mcfeelys.com

MY LAMP PARTS
3540 N. Spaulding
Chicago, IL 60618
773-539-7910
www.mylampparts.com

RADIO SHACK
300 RadioShack Circle
Fort Worth, TX 76102-1964
800-843-7422
www.radioshack.com

**ROCKLER WOODWORKING
AND HARDWARE**
4365 Willow Dr.
Medina, MN 55340
800-279-4441
www.rockler.com

THE HOME DEPOT
2455 Paces Ferry Rd.
Atlanta, GA 30339
800-466-3337
www.homedepot.com

WINDY RIDGE WOODWORKS
6751 Hollenbach Rd,
New Tripoli, PA 18066
www.wrwoodworks.com
*Instruction, Fine Furniture, Advice
and Encouragement*

WOODCRAFT SUPPLY LLC
1177 Rosemar Rd.
P.O. Box 1686
Parkersburg, WV 26102
800-535-4482
www.woodcraft.com

WOODWORKER'S HARDWARE
P.O. Box 180
Sauk Rapids, MN 56379-0180
800-383-0130
www.wwhardware.com

WOODWORKER'S SUPPLY
1108 N. Glenn Rd.
Casper, WY 82601
800-645-9292
www.woodworker.com

Ideas. Instruction. Inspiration.

These and other great **Popular Woodworking** products are available at your local bookstore, woodworking store or online supplier.

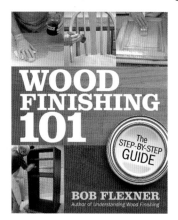

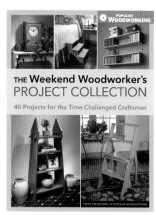

WOOD FINISHING 101
By Bob Flexner
Wood finishing doesn't have to be complicated or confusing. Wood Finishing 101 boils it down to simple step-by-step instructions and pictures on how to finish common woods using widely-available finishing materials. Bob Flexner has been writing about and teaching wood finishing for over 20 years.

paperback • 128 pages

WEEKEND WOODWORKER'S PROJECT COLLECTION
This book has 40 projects from which to choose and, depending on the level of your woodworking skills, any of them can be completed in one or two weekends. Projects include: a game box, jewelry box, several styles of bookcases and shelves, mirrors, picture frames and more.

paperback • 256 pages

POPULAR WOODWORKING MAGAZINE
Whether learning a new hobby or perfecting your craft, *Popular Woodworking Magazine* has expert information to teach the skill, not just the project. Find the latest issue on newsstands, or you can order online at popularwoodworking.com.

SHOPCLASS VIDEOS
From drafting, to dovetails and even how to carve a ball-and-claw foot, our Shop Class Videos let you see the lesson as if you were standing right there.

Available at shopwoodworking.com
DVD & Instant download

POPULAR WOODWORKING'S VIP PROGRAM

Get the Most Out of Woodworking!

Join the Woodworker's Bookshop VIP program today for the tools you need to advance your woodworking abilities. Your one-year paid renewal membership includes:

• *Popular Woodworking Magazine* (1 year/7 issue U.S. subscription — A $21.97 Value)

• *Popular Woodworking Magazine CD* — Get all issues of *Popular Woodworking Magazine* from 2006 to today on one CD (A $64.95 Value!)

• The Best of Shops & Workbenches CD — 62 articles on workbenches, shop furniture, shop organization and the essential jigs and fixtures published in *Popular Woodworking* and *Woodworking Magazine* ($15.00 Value!)

• 20% Members-Only Savings on 6-Month Subscription for Shop Class OnDemand

• 10% Members-Only Savings at Shopwoodworking.com

• 10% Members-Only Savings on FULL PRICE Registration for Woodworking In America Conference (Does Not Work with Early Bird Price)

• and more....

Visit **popularwoodworking.com** to see more woodworking information by the experts, learn about our digital subscription and sign up to receive our weekly newsletter at popularwoodworking.com/newsletters/

  FOLLOW POPULAR WOODWORKING